YOU LOOK LIKE
SOMETHING BLOOMING

"You have to own your own joy and wonder so that no matter what someone does or doesn't do, you still have some left inside." —India Ame'ye

YOU LOOK LIKE

Something Blooming

India Ame'ye

A Memoir of Divination Seeds to
Cultivate Your Feminine Garden Temple

—

"My heart has become a bird which searches in the sky. Every part of me goes in different directions. Is it really so that the one I love is everywhere?" -Rumi

—

Dance in the mornings to the sound of sun. Get your body used to being in the flow of movement.
-India Ame'ye

Second Edition —The Second Coming or The 2nd Cummin' (You Choose)
Modern Woman, Indigenous Spirit Press

© 2014, 2015 by India Ame'ye.
All rights reserved.

Cover photo © by India Ame'ye
Cover Art by SenseThePoint
Interior photos © by India Ame'ye

Modern Woman, Indigenous Spirit Press
Fairfield, Iowa

"Every creative has a dark space from where her/his/their creation flows; a

bottomless abyss of mystery; invisible in its visibility. Harnessed and deeply

strapped. Darkness giving rise to the light of dawn. Cloaked with love; rising

and shining as love. Shadows and emotional depth sparking condensed light.

Dark matter that sings psalms deliciously offbeat. Hooded in healing and

regenerative power. Extensions into your deepest harmony, greatest alignment,

and truth. It's within vulnerability that one accesses this sacred and cosmic

information and rebirth their whole selves into new and brighter light. Go into

the dark, veil up sun-being. At worst, dark and light are mere allies. At best they

are simply

ONE."

--India Ame'ye

Say you are gorgeous
and mean what you say!

Cheers, India

Bloom

noun —The condition of being a flower
verb —1) To support plant life. 2) To shine and glow. 3) A state or time of beauty, freshness, and vigor

Synonyms—
Blossom : Open : Floret : Bud : Flourish : Essence : Allure : To receive without shame or fear|**The sacred initiation into ......becoming**

Warm Sun:

I play unfettered in the forest, and oftentimes I go alone. I always come back into the world more rejuvenated and clearer than I left. I like to observe nature, especially when no one else is around. Today I saw the largest turtle ever and a group of birds playing a song, but they didn't sound like birds. The pitch of their enchantment had humanlike qualities. And I was there. Alone. Quiet. Taking visual notes on how to live/love/dream and imagining myself as a better human spirit. *How can I learn to embody more love, I wondered.*

I like to explore creeks, falls, snakes, birds, rocks, dirt, leaves and trees. and I talk to everything because I feel presence within everything. It's all alive. Yep I greet the forest before entering just like I'd greet another person. I trust nature; I give up my worry and live out my safety. To travel on foot miles into the forest.
Alone.

I show my self, sometimes my whole self to natural the natural world because it it's a different eye into myself. Today I was back up in MAMA EARTH, surrounded by earth, not another person in sight. Everything looked so magical and dreamy so I delightfully removed my clothes and did sun salutations. I feel like clothes trap harmful energy into our skins, tissues, and bones. And sweeping my total body in nature not only moves the energy, it shows nature that I trust it to heal, love, and protect me. It responds to my thoughts/vibrations accordingly.

~Notes from journal (2006)~The beginning of my beginnings~

"One of the most potent charms you can give a lover/partner is total and complete trust in what his/her feelings are without any need to process a thing."

- The Devotee Archetype~

TABLE OF CONTENTS

Please note: 'You Look Like Something Blooming' is not entirely a how-to, self-help book. Instead it is fresh literary juice to encourage readers to dig deeper into their own lives, implant different experiences, and drink in more love, harmony, and abundance in every area of their lives. It encourages readers to get excited about the capacities and possibilities for their own lives. Be very clear, we are here —in these bodies—-simply to love. So I wrote a book that brings everything back to love. The harvest is upon us because it has always been <u>within</u> us, waiting for us to simply receive and burst open in full bloom.

'"You Look Like Something Blooming" seeds sustainable loving back into our bodies, lives, and the living Earth. The feminine and intimate arts: From theory into practice.

#1 Tip for reading this book:
You don't have to believe anything that is written within these pages.

"Look Mum. I wrote my first book."
—India Ame'ye, age 7 (true story)

In loving memory of Mum, she who taught me to sing into my skin while putting on lotion.

"Falling out of love is really falling out of alignment with your deepest truth. " -India Ame'ye

Halo Beloved. Before we deep sea dive into the inner world, may I share some holy scripture with you? Please consider placing these words between your warm thighs:

If you have a headache, find the deeper remedy as soon as possible. If you have cramps, find relief as soon as possible. If your heart aches, find some soothing sweetness when you have moved through your emotions—as soon as possible. Essentially you don't want your body to get accustomed to being in pain as a normal way of existing.

""Many women have been tricked out of their softness, inaccurately led to believe that it equates to weakness and docility. But a soft woman doesn't necessarily mean a fragmented woman. There's actually great strength in the irresistible softness of femininity. While she knows how to yield and surrender when necessary, a soft woman could be leading a pack a wolves and not be noticed. Plus she's got the charm to make others think they are actually leading, but gently and most lovingly, they are indeed being led."
— OSHUN'S DAUGHTERS BY INDIA AME'YE"

"Between your *thighs* is generous plant life. Think about it."
—India Ame'ye

A MESSAGE FROM THE AUTHOR

TILTING YOUR HEAD BACK WHILE MOANING THE SACRED SOUND "AHHH" ENSURES THAT YOUR THROAT IS OPEN AND THE ENERGIES YOU SPEAK AFTERWARDS CUM FROM THE DIRECT CHANNEL OF YOUR HEART. NO MATTER HOW SOMETHING MAY SOUND TO ANOTHER, YOU ARE SPEAKING YOUR TRUTH FROM AN EMBODIED ECSTASY CALLED LOVE. EVENTUALLY A PERSON GETS ACCUSTOMED THAT YOU ARE IN YOUR TRUTH ONLY BECAUSE YOU BECOME MORE COMFORTABLE WITH WHO/WHAT YOU ARE AT THE CORE OF YOUR BEING. HOW LOVELY THAT HUMANITY MERELY REFLECTS BACK, BY WAY OF THEIR EXPERIENCES WITH YOU, WHATEVER IT IS YOU TRULY BELIEVE ABOUT YOURSELF OR (YOUR 'CELLVES').

"AHHH" was imbued with the divine responsibility to assist women in coming into alignment and perfect harmony with the natural connection to our bodies, to the earth, to our hearts, and to the infinite spirit of pleasure. I accepted this sacred call through writing my first charming book, "You Look Like Something Blooming: A Memoir of Divination Seeds to Cultivate Your Feminine Garden Temple."

But I did NOT just write a book, oh no warm Light-beings, I answered a call. I became a conduit for information to flow into me then out of me and into anyone I encountered. The transformative power that being present in one's body unearths, and how it seeds and ripples transformation into others by way of simply being in the energy—mind, body, and spirit. The transformation began from building my connection with nature, and from there spending whole days in orgasm, sometimes crying orgasms or bursting full body sensations. I learned how to listen, to enhance my magnetism (point of attraction), reframe and rewrite my stories, and ignite healing in my organs and life. I am now at the point in my life where I can say what I want, and by the power of my expectation, whatever I desire—blooms. A living wand in command of life. Confidently flowing through the forests, embodying fairy energy, and collecting little blooms along the way, blooms that are inside the creases of this spellbook.

Through language, pictures, poems, moans, musings, and wildness, I delightfully share my journey into the spirit of love from a feminine perspective and integrative wholeness (inner masculine).

Taste this: I write the words "pussy," "yoni," and "vagina"; please don't get too caught up in semantics though. Just take sips and let it drizzle out the corners of your mouth. While these words are very similar and interrelated, the conjure and connection of each word is radically different. So when I translate my life in this book, I write the way it came up. The deeper reality is that within the darkness of the womb, the greatest and grandest mystery, _all_ is accepted, available, and _adored._ Your inner ocean has the capacity to take whatever's given and reconstruct it into the fabrics of your cells. So give it love as often as you remember to do so. Consider moving away from much of what you have been taught about these words, and just feel into the syllables and sounds. If you don't understand, don't worry about understanding; simply keep trying to feel into your pussy. See how that works? If you feel emotional, congrats— simply keep going deeper into what you feel. The vagina is the portal of the divine. Yoni magic is the playpen of manifestation. The embodied love, the darkest night, the wet and wetter, the foggiest moment, the mist and misery, the lush and yum, the juice out of an activated ass, the completion of that project, those seeds and incoming babies, the creations and destructions, come from the same Source.

Smell This Beloved: _Sit with your legs open for entry, as if you know that you have the power to not only dissolve the patterns, beliefs, and conditions of the Old paradigm inflicted upon your body, but the clear watery capacity to create a vision for the sustainable New Paradigm by way of your Being and Living it._

11

Making fresh juice with it. Strengthen your back with it. Time to practice what you already know, what you were brave enough to recall from your deepest knowings, and let it ripple into your life, love, and community.

Ode to mystical, incense-burning pussy

PROLOGUE

For the woman who said she'd pray for me...

How dare you
with your judgments and projections
determine whether another person's life, lover(s), or ways of being
are 'good' or 'bad?'
What God, Buddha, or Jesus gave you dominion
over what is 'right' or 'wrong' for anyone else?

Don't pray for others unless requested to do so.
Otherwise you are poking holes in people's personal spaces
to be beautifully who and where they are.
Pray for the courage to love others however they show up.
Pray to remember that people have the right to be how they are...
and it's not necessary for you to understand any of it.
Sacred and/or profane.
Magical and wild.
Unconventional and proud.
Wild and wandering.
Wood nymphs, harlots, wizards, fairies, and medicine women
transforming anger and stagnation into creative action.
Activating body temples. Not wearing clothing,
instead wearing their bodies as clothing.
Wet. daily. like. flowers.

Don't judge another person's emotional space.
Pray for the life force to be reminded that there is no emotional
hierarchy,
Only emotional authenticity.
Pray for the bravery to remember that what you see in another
reflects back to how you truly see yourself.
Pray for sight to truly see.

Pray for the love and strength to deeply listen to another
without being so readied to speak.
Don't pray for me.
Pray for a harness large enough to transfer
high levels of creative energy into your anus, the area that houses
your root chakra, your safety, freedom, and consciousness.
Pray that you can be vulnerable enough
to allow full body orgasms as only
the BEGINNING of a lovemaking experience.
Pray to recall from the depths of your womb
that all experiences are divine and purposeful.

Don't pray for me. Pray for your beloved.
You as your beloved. Pray for you.

Pray For Your Blooming

*"I am brave enough
to channel the fierce audacity
necessary to live my life
as one sustained, unappropriated orgasm."*

—India Ame'ye

Are you drinking tap water because you are catching up to your financial abundance that
will allow you to afford pure alkaline water in a glass jar? Don't worry you'll catch up. In
the meantime, add 1 tspn of apple cider vinegar (the brand has the mother in it|read the
label) to your tap water. The acv helps to purify the water and immediately raises its
alkalinity. Drink out of glass jars as much as possible. If your lips are often dry/cracked,
just sip on more **alkaline** water. Deliver moisture into your cells and into every area of
your life as a result.

FEMININE VOICE BELONGS TO US ALL

"Before getting out of bed, I like to open my warm throat and engage my moans. Moaning in the morning sets a pleasurable tone for the day ahead. Ahhh, Ahhh, ahhh darlin'. And everyone around me just gets used to a woman being inside grand ecstasy outside the context of another person person. Meditative Seeds Subconsciously Planted. To unearth. The Courage. To Engage Their Unique Psalms. Sans Guilt, Shame, or Fear." --India Ame'ye

"AHHH" speak with a deeply rooted feminine voice. I conjure through the medium of language and wild images with a mind dominant in feminine thought as a feminine archetype. I am deeply intimate with nature, which essentially is the grandest intimacy with myself and the whole of existence. I write my life... but with that, my language has its limitations because I tend to write how I receive ... yet the spirit of what's being expressed can touch any person open to wildness and orgasmic living, self-healing (the source of collective healing), igniting body magic and internal healing, and discovering *very simple and practical* ways of tapping into her/his/their personal freedom, regardless of said person's gender and sexuality expressions. My language is useful for ANY person interested in evolving from old outdated programs and conditioning around what the human body is capable of experiencing. My voice and mind disseminate information for ALL people, any person who affirms his/her/their energy as feminine or even occasionally feminine, for those who find themselves attracted to us, and anyone who leans outside all of it.

DEFINITION OF FEMININITY

In case you skipped the 1ˢᵗ few pages lets review this again: Tilting your head back while moaning the sacred sound "AHHH" ensures that your throat is open and the word-energies you speak afterwards cum from the direct channel of your heart.

"Everyone born into modern culture learns how to be masculine from birth. Now we remember what it is like to be feminine and emerge, not fragmented or incomplete, but as whole beings, ebbing and flowing, waxing and waning, sashaying inside of greater harmony and collective nourishment."

- Dance of Symbiosis, India Ame'ye

FEMININITY IS "AHHH" **courageous act**—essentially the courage to **receive**— feeling worthy of receiving, whether from humanity or the cosmic collective. Femininity is the **divine yield**- the ability to navigate harmony and ease where ever you are in life, realizing that harmony is only an external manifestation of what is taking place inside your body temple. Femininity is tender power — the capacity to tap into ancient practices in order to love better, relate better, heal, and evolve. Femininity is **possibility**—the ability to command life to be whatever it is that you desire for it to be because you are armed with all sorts of SIMPLE magical tools (being) and divine application (doing/action) to command life. How a person's moves and operates in the feminine archetype looks differently for everyone and thankfully so— as ALL expressions of femininity are necessary and essential to provide balance for the whole.

Perhaps it's clear by now that the human body is a construction of complements: Adam/Eve, Mother/Father, Virgin Mary/Mary Magdalene, light and dark. Everything/Nothing. Yin/Yang, Masculine/Feminine. Therefore the human body at its best is wholeness. With that understanding there is a sacred call and massive necessity to cultivate FEMININE ENERGY, tilling the energy out of nutrient-deficit soil into greater light and fuller blooms. How can you be of service?

I write extensively about feminine energy, partly because of the confusion, bewilderment, and turmoil surrounding this **brave medicine**. Most people process life through a masculine lens only—that's the confusion we learn and operate within. Many women were taught the illusions of femininity, and like their mothers, find themselves imbalanced, tired with heavy periods and other womb issues, lacking the tools and wisdom to procure magic and miracles, and predominately existing outside of ease and pleasure. Believe it or not, intentionally cultivating feminine energy blooms greater balance into our bodies, lives, and planet.

First let's distinguish feminine energy from a learned feminine presence, which tells women to cross our legs, wear make-up and high heels, and get our hair and nails done. By the way, I love those external *learned* representations of femininity sometimes. But feminine energy is the soft, yielding, mysterious, quiet spaces within. Loud and intentional, slow and deliberate, transformative (destructive/ like a tsunami or Kali/ disorganized and frazzled). Nourishing, wild, wise, intuitive, organized and tidy, messy and chaotic, multi-orgasmic, healthy, abundant, and healing magic within. Feminine energy is the inner medicine woman who knows the many uses of aloe, burdock root, and sexual connection. Believe it or not, some of our great grandmas were probably quite feminine-energetically driven!

Cultivating feminine energy is connecting to the magic & mystery of your very existence. It's embracing all of life's experiences with an inner smile and deep knowingness that at the very core of your nature, you are balanced, whole, God/Goddess reincarnate, and connected to everything around you. You are nature. You are love and sensuality. You are the cosmic collective.

You are the greatest transformation. And from this sacred space, you *can* call forth your inner masculine in the outward reflection of another person (a lover or lovers) and/or pursue transformation in your life. Nothing is separate and all is connected because true transformation can ONLY come from accepting responsibility for life's experiences. How can we truly change ANYTHING outside of ourselves is the greater point. *One of the biggest breakthroughs I encountered in 39 years alive in this healthy body temple was that wholeness is achieved through balancing the masculine and feminine within the self first. Relationship and partnerships can not be expected substitute for the lack of inner balance meaning lack wholeness in the self.*

I am here, Great Goddess. Utilize me. Utilize these charged breasts, sweet lips, sensitive thighs, and djembe-beating heart ..utilize them. Teach me to cultivate my sacred geometry as you express yourself through me. I am spread ass wide open, summoning the full moon into my body. Our bodies. Bodies of water. Ancient and recent bodies. Old and young bodies. Dragon and fairy bodies. All bodies that came from the mysteries of one woman. Bowed deeply with my ass facing the moon. Clapped my cheeks in standing ovation. Such an honor to adore myself in these moment. To cleanse my anus (root), stir my sacral fire, and ignite my spine! To cleanse the collective anus, to stir collective fire, and to ignite the collective spine. May there be peace throughout the the body of creation. One love, one heart, one being, one body.

~Blooming Tip~

The luminous presence of the mystical womb informs the physical womb, not the other way around. A forgotten source of power that rests between the container of the hips connected to the psyche and life, glowing outwardly and lighting the ancient ways of healing and manifestation (or wombifestion). With that consideration women who have had hysterectomies have the capacity to play as well. They too can embrace their potential energetic capacities and groove to the impending harmonies, manifestations, and transformations.

"How?" She purred.

1. Consider purchasing a yoni egg. There's a wealth of information online about these earth jewels worn inside your pussy and how they activate your healing and pleasure.

2. Steaming your yoni portal. More information on yoni steams on page 135.
3. Talk to your Beloved. Your pussy as your Beloved. Get to know your depth, viscosity, sounds, taste, texture, and smells. Use a hand mirror and get warm and wet over your learnings and discoveries.

Wondering what on earth blooming tips are? Blooming tips are highlights that enabled my personal transformation into being a Living Goddess. Here's the 2nd one below:

Blooming Tip

Many relationships (or at least how we LEARN to relate as lovers) are attracted to substitute for the void we have within ourselves (our 'cellves'). An abundance of stress goes into the cells (the organs) to keep, hold, block, restrict, fragment, and sustain. But when one dares to explore her/his/their whole self, there is no void. And when there is no void, there can only be pure love, which means space, agency, freedom, truth, and growth even inside beautiful and brilliant monogamous connections. As a queer woman affirmed in my femininity, I saw the necessity to explore all the parts of me, to give honorable mention to my whole self, without question or concern. The exploration has made me more of a natural magnet to joy and puts less pressure on another person (or situation) to be the impetus to that joy via our connection and experiences. Even if my stride leans light years deeply and celestially into the feminine, I am still whole and accessible to the ALL that lives within me, available and connected to that Oneness. A living body of Earth sauntering up a desolate dirt road in a lace sweater and yoga pants with my breasts bouncing out of my sweater, and somehow, nothing is missing. One foot in front of the other, high stepping as an abundance of love, that which is interconnected with the ALL, without question or concern. It is surely some brand of activism, accessible to ALL, without question or concern. It doesn't mean that I'm not wildly charmed by compassionate masculinity, but it does mean that my spirit needed to access what it meant and continues to mean to be whole first (to the best of my ability). To nourish my inner masculine God alongside my feminine to the best of my abilities.

"The womb is the altar upon which energy is transformed into matter. Sit, pray, and utilize it."
-India Ame'ye

My Dark Goddess Invocation

I was always afraid to observe within myself that I was a Dark Goddess, some-how I was strangled in the human disillusion that anything "dark" meant "bad," "evil," or "tainted." The dis-ease of good vs bad or right vs wrong and bending myself to fit into musty boxes of "good and right" perceptions and condition-ings. It wasn't until a powerful dear friend randomly called me a "Triple Dark Goddess" that I allowed those words to warm me open and have their way. Turned into a wet sea over the beauty and potency. Uninhibitedly and unapolo-getically sweet and loving, courteous, thoughtful, playful, nature fairy childlike, gentle yet profoundly connected to darkness as ONE. The ancestors, death, and the underworld, snakes and kundalini, bats and mystery, heat and fire, smoke and ecstasy, conjuring and word-power-sound, potatoes, pumpkins (root veg-gies) and manifestation, herbal medicine and apothecary, the alchemy within my yoni, the abundance within my ass (root), breasts (heart), lungs (breath), and heart, the brilliancy of re-creation and destruction (essentially less living in the past, more presence in the now moment), brave solitude, and of course commu-nication with my deepest mystery which is the warmth, creation, and nature liv-ing inside my womb, shall I go on?! My spirit came 'here' suited in reddish-black to blueish-black skin-tones depending on my level of sun penetration and moon reflection to express itself through balanced divine femininity and integrative wholeness. Breasts rotating on the axis of my heart while being commanded to point at the sky as some otherworldly mythology. Speaking of command, I also command my safety inside my anus that no human, animal, or energy desires to harm me, so there's no need for protection.... for me. I just keep Earth inside of me, spinning red flowers from within. Throat open, activating dark matter as DNA, veiled out with my ass (root) tooted in the air. Out-of-doors, a living tree you may sense, affirming that I'm not fragmented, but dark, loving, gentle, and whole. Mysteriously tapped into the greatest abundance: freedom. Howling the names of Olokun, Oya, and Kali when it's necessary without any awareness that I am even doing so. Like I'm merely scratching an itch.

~Intermission, Beloved ~

Maybe stop what you're doing ....and go make a smoothie right now. If it's within your harmony, add vegetables. Learn how to drink your fruits and veggies without always hav-ing to add sweeteners: stevia, honey, or sugar. Your body has less work to do when your food is already in liquid form and a better chance at deeply receiving the nutrients.

NUTRIENT-RICH SOIL

Let your titties all the way out. Witness your chest rise and fall as you breathe in the seedlings. Take your time with each page. Like life, "You Look Like Something Blooming" is random, unpredictable, imperfect yet a madly, deeply *purrfect, heart-opening, literary salve. Like life, there will be typos.*

*Purposely nonlinear, sans order as feminine energy at its **peak** doesn't follow order or guidelines. Like a highly orgasmic women, off-center, off-beat, open, available. It's quite purposeful that the mind has to pay close attention to what's being communicated and not just simply fill in the blanks because it knows that alphabetically A comes after B and B comes before C.*

*"You Look Like Something Blooming" doesn't play those lazy, mental games. It's a book that commands you to **be** inside your glorious body temple, shook up, laughing, startled blushing, cummin' and crying.....*

Because you never know what you are going to get when you turn the page. Within the randomness lies tremendous harmony. An ode to life.

So grab your moon-charged water, tea, juice, and/or holy vodka. Get ready to bask in the upcoming harvest. Are you feeling your waters yet?

Every seed written in each line is useful for healing, empowerment, transformation, and the yum of the whole existence.

If it's within your harmony, treat each page as a tarot card, divination, or meditation. Randomly flip through a page or pages, observe what comes up for you, and journal, sing, chant to invite the information to deeply penetrate your organs.

Ahhhhhh (throat open) --giggles--

Let's begin ... again.

SEEDS

I

In the beginning...

Adam and Eve, the unification of the divine masculine and divine feminine -one being, one body- were "naked" meaning they were (spaceless, ageless, timeless, authentic, vulnerable ... cunning, conscious, aware ... and felt no shame or pretension! (Gen 2:25) In the beginning, Adam and Eve danced in the fertile womb and tinkered with magic daily.

 Cunning is magic; It is the power we all have to manipulate energy and matter. When harnessed with love, you become a transformative healer and can command life by pointing your finger, a living wand. You become a deity in a short skirt walking down Magazine Street. Some call it God, Goddess, Oshun, stardust, or even just plain ol' strange. But it doesn't matter what you call it, simply delight in doing the sacred work to unlock your unique code and access your unique energy to transform your life.

II

Life will deliciously happen, but it's not happening *to you, it's happening through you, through those worship-able and wet thighs, you co-creator you.* Things won't always go as planned. Life will even get a bit messy and painstakingly emotional. You will cry a river out of your eyes, nose, and throat. But how you process life and the accompanying experiences will indicate your capacity to heal and tap into greater freedom that will most indubitably transform your life. Good news is that you have two options: You either process life inside limitations or inside abundance, perceiving all experiences as setbacks or setups for growth and evolution. Neither way is better than the other, but both yield radically different outcomes.

> The main theme within me is African, but I am a child of the earth so where ever I go, I am home ... nurtured, nourished, cared for, at ease, and 100 percent supported. I never need 'protection.' This earth is all up inside my body, a living Organism. I breathe, it breathes. It breathes, I receive.

"Life translates a bit easier when everything I owned fit inside two suitcases and one carry-on. Life feels lighter, wider, breathable, and receivable." -India Ame'ye, after giving away over 400 books, 15 bags of clothes, shoes, and costumes, and a crate of records with accompanying record player

Just start to think like  you are magic. Get the magic inside your head. Through the back door of your tongue and down into your throat. Soon you will start to feel that you are indeed magic and synchronicities, incantations, and unusual possibilities will show up with the point of your pinky finger.

~The abundant promise|Bunny hopping through the day~

Blooming Tip

Think bigger, beyond the human constructs of ethnicity, gender, and consider de-centering money. Sure these constructions can be calls for celebration and wild praise at times, however you don't have to be bound by ethnicity and gender nor base decisions, attractions, relocation possibilities, worth, financial goals, health expectations, or body capabilities around any of it. Remember you are spirit first, this sexy human body temple is only but a container for you to experience the senses and actualize a sensuous human existence. Don't get trapped into childhood learnings and expectations. Listen to the strangest sounds, watch silent films, sky-dive, tell others you have booked a trip overseas (even if you can't locate your money), make up your own language and stories, consider your body as otherworldly, open your ass cheeks to the light of the moon, and witness your transformations.

Consider having a fertile body, regardless of whether or not you want to have babies. The adult human body is 60-75% water so it's pretty clear how necessary it is to intake watery-rich foods, juices, and herbal teas. Cucumbers, watermelons, *freshly-pressed* vegetables and fruit juices, grapefruit, oranges, dandelion tea, and the like.
Because
.....a **juicy** woman
is a..... healthy, fertile woman.
And fertility, health, and abundance are all synonymous.

Drink in the juice of fertility.
Then become healthier and far more abundant
in the next moment.

She said to her aching lover, "May I cleanse your soul's
wounds with my female ejaculate?"

IV

Do you know that your gorgeous breasts can be power lines to the divine? **Be open to them being sucked, fucked, and prayed upon.** Be open to the body's capacity to heal itself and another. Be open to vulnerability, silence, awkward most uncomfortable moments, farting in bed, laughter as tears (releasing), weird sounds cummin out of your body, receiving, trancing, climaxing and more ... at any given moment. Be open to ecstatic, untamed, wild, transformative experiences.... Having your mind blown in unconventional, healing ways. Be open to going in and out of consciousness where your lover evolves into her or his healer self. Be open to moaning, peace, cursing, quiet, loud, country ass, raw encounters and realize that all is sacred when affirmed as such and not just because the Bible says so. Be open to your capacity to be someone else's medicine and receiving the same offering. Be open to lovers as mirrors, where they are never made to believe that they are "wrong" or "guilty" only embraced for their growth, difference, and calls for more love. Be open to full body orgasms, where one lover climaxes energizes and opens another lover's heart. Be open to releasing programs on what love should feel like or look like ... and embrace what lies before you, with arms and legs wide open drawing in unlimited pleasure for the greater good of the planet. One year and eight months of celibacy taught me the depths of receptivity and unconditional love and how being open to sexual pleasure and intimacy is less about "doing" but more so about "being." Surrendering the Past. Feeling. Receiving. And deeply trusting the love that stares back. Be open while it is alive and present before you. **The world needs all women to come into alignment with their sensual pleasure.** *How can you help?*

 be open: omens of the Great Mother

V

Contemplate being an altar for someone else.

A sacred place where one can lay her/his heart down, be heard
without interruption, held without concern, and simply transformed
by your healing presence. If another person is healing, so are you.
When you nourish yourself with the highest quality of foods, juices,
and water, it is not just for you, but also for the collective. That
person you heal through connection via your nourished body temple
will go out into the world and heal someone else, maybe you ... in
return.

 Body Altars—The necessity for nourished body temples

Blooming Tip: You were taught from birth how to give, now harness the courage to learn how to receive.

Every human body has varying degrees of feminine (receiver) and
masculine (giver) energy, therefore, everybody is worthy of
receiving. An intimate couple has to decide who is the "giver" and
who is the "receiver" for optimal healing purposes. A conversation
doesn't necessarily have to happen with words. It can be decided
based upon energy, connection, and being aware of what each
other's needs are at any particular time. Women who identify as
butch or masculine leaning may want to consider being receivers
sometimes. Masculine men who resist being receivers may want to
challenge their fears and resistance sometimes. People who dance
outside of gender or inside all genders may want to consider being
receivers sometimes. *Even many women who are highly feminine*

presenting have a hard time receiving. The ability to receive, to take the medicine inside the organs, the tender spaces that house the emotions, nourishes the body back into integrity and wholeness. The opportunity to be laid back, engaging your moans, and doing absolutely nothing else is the prescription. To be touched and explored with healing, prayers, and incantations without anything being said. To be kissed, fondled, sucked, lapped, kneaded, and rode into warm submission without anything being said. The fragmented feminine placed back into wholeness without anything being said. The fragmented Earth indubitably positioned back into wholeness without anything (ever) being said.

This feeling. Ferocious, swollen, and raw. Unceasingly vigorous and explosive. Barefoot and all-natural. Wet. A nourishing, knife-sharp necessity for one single moment. Feral in hormones and pheromones. Feral in water and fire. Feral in spirit and spit. Feral in sweat and sweetness. Feral in depth and mystery. Feral in smoke and ecstasy. Don't bring your illusive, learned constructions of safety. Don't bring an unbalanced ego and lack of freedom. Don't bring one single limitation on love. Bring your pure innocence, pure passion, the warm sun on your naked body. Bring your primal allegiance to softness and moisture. Bring your hunger for mystery and these thick thighs. I want to see you drink from the clearest hot spring. Bend me over until there's nothing left but crusts of mud underneath my fingernails. Paws and purrs. Slippin', slidin', and motor-boatin' into the next in-breath. Cosmically ordained to immerse ourselves into one another's afterglow. Someday.

-California

Springtime is so luscious and surely isn't the culprit of your allergies. The culprit of your allergies is **you** accompanied by your diet of synthetic grains (gluten), heavily pasteurized dairy, refined sugary snacks, and foods fried in highly acidic oils. Also lack of water and fresh juices, and herbal teas. And you can't just make a shift for one month, it has to be a total overall lifestyle change. A permanent way of living...and loving...you..and anyone who encounters you. Try lemon+ cucumber water + fasting for 7 days on fruits and vegetables. Then go outside and play.

VI

Do you know that women can cultivate our curves with our thoughts? That's ONE of the many powers of our brilliant mind. The mind isn't an autopilot machine! We have the power to command our mind to be used in any way we desire. As Goddesses (spirit beings) gliding the Earth's grid in our feminine graces, we can command trees to sway, wind to dance around leaves, or birds to sing sweet, high vibrational lullabies in our royal honor. As deeply rich and powerful as we are, we can summon seemingly inanimate objects to rise on our behalf. Sure this could sound silly to some, and that perception is valid and OK, but belief + action = transformation.

I adore drawing from my personal experiences. When using the mind as a learning tool, I can receive all types of information on how my body works and how to move energy throughout it, similarly to how energy moves throughout the planets and cosmos. As stars masquerading as human spirits, we can tap more into ourselves by understanding how nature operates, survives, and thrives.

This ancient information brought into the modern world has

helped me to maximize my time so that even exercising has become less about sculpting and toning my body and more about INVITING the most PLEASURABLE energy into my crown chakra and third eye portals on the inhale, and using the exhale to glide the energy throughout my heart, navel, sacral, yoni, anus, and up my spine. This internal alchemy cleanses my organs, stores extra energy into my navel center, and enhances my orgasmic potential.

With the aid of visualizations, reprogramming, and reframing stories I tell myself over and over again, I can create and re-create tone and curves too.

...My aunt Gemma taught me what a round ass and curvy body do for humanity...

Cultivating energy flow or learning how to cycle energy throughout the body enhances every area of a woman's life, especially intimacy and sex. The reason why a woman's energy doesn't flow i.e. (she doesn't orgasm; she doesn't 'feel' easily; she's not easily aroused/ excited) typically originates in childhood. Many little girls are scolded into not allowing energy to flow into their pelvis, not to touch themselves, not to act too sensual, or not to feel sensations in their pussies. Of course most girls are made to feel that sex is dirty or not to be talked about, and that "good girls" don't think about or have sex. Girls then spend so much time, years, tensing their pelvic muscles and ignoring any sensation they feel "down there," and learn not to pay much attention to their "vaginas" that they literally close themselves off from pleasure, even simple pleasures e.g. basking in sunshine or singing songs out of their registers, or furiously dancing. Some parents then use the Bible to further repress children's feelings and sensations, resulting in all types of mental, emotional, and spiritual BLOCKAGES. These blockages manifest in the emotional body and transfer into the physical body of repressed, un-pleasable, non-orgasmic adults. Cultivating energy flow creates a pleasurable life, and helps one to understand that pleasure creates contagious joy, because when you feel delicious, you can transfer that deliciousness onto someone else. *mmm, tasty oneness*

I'll be even more transparent... learning how to cycle energy throughout my body saved my life. Stagnant energy creates tumors and diseases in the human body, and every woman in my (birth) family has/had tumors, fibroids, or some type of cancer or heart dis-ease ... until I decided to re-create my family STORIES and transform my life.

*Women are water and the healthiest bodies of water
MOVE, MOVE, and MOVE. BREATHE, FEEL,
ALLOW, RELEASE, and repeat. Be like WATER, wait,
you are Water!
As such just stay juicy!*

Blooming Tip: Rewriting Stories
(From Victim to Creator)
Possible Trigger for Any Person with Molestation Sensitivities

I was born a healer, lover, and minister, long before I got the degrees, certificates, and accolades. Even as a child I honored my powers and abilities to make powerful choices that impacted my life and landed me on my feet as an adult in two-inch, functional heels, bright-eyed and healthy with impeccable digestion. At 6 years, I healed a grown man with my blooming body. He needed touch and I was available. He needed my ministry and I was there. I have learned to trust my life and all the ways in which I place my imprint upon it. I have learned to ignite my powers by taking divine ownership for everything that happened *through* me, NOT

TO ME, including on that warm summer day in 1981. I needed that experience without question or concern, because it taught me at 6 years old that adults need more love. Adults need more touch, like babies. If not, they will continue to fill up with dis-ease and die un-lived and tapped out. Life isn't random. I have not been a victim. And I hold the template for how I live and whom I love, and I loved him, wept for him, because two years later, he died at age 30. And here I am, 31 years later, embodying love, twirling in love, and loving-- with every beat of my open heart.

* I have no idea what happened to him, but how beautiful and brilliant this story is and how wonderfully powerful it resonates in my body every time I revisit it in my visions or words. Energizing my *new* story healed my organs and the triggers, pain, and dis-eases therein. I set my whole self ... *free.* Now you can go pondering "what if that happens" or "what if this happens" until you dry up from the inside out, but eventually you get to the point within your magic that when a person is 'dead' to you, then they are just that. And you just move on.

Blooming Tip: Move as if you have the whole world inside your hips, because you do.

"Don't be satisfied with stories, how things have gone with others. Unfold your own myth."
— Rumi

"Because even in silence, you hear exquisite sound."
—India Ame'ye

VII

Every damn time
I have sex,
I cry. Not
because something is
wrong,
but because everything is
right!
And days later, my ass
gets full,
fatter with love and de-light.

Receivers, transmitters, and spiritual (sexual) beings: The consequences of being human

Blooming Tips

Sex and/or sexually simulated movements activate ass and thighs to come alive with ease and pleasure. Sexually simulated movements such as belly-dancing, twerking, or squats.

The feminine blooms in the mystery and quiet. Tap into your silence and inner stillness and witness more calm, ease, and nourishing flavors happen in your life.

VIII (POSSIBLE TRIGGER FOR ANYONE WITH SENSITIVITIES TO ILLNESS)

Be courageous enough to
dismantle the blueprint
stored in your body as a child.
It's killing you.
Be brave enough to regain
access to your own body.
It will heal you.

Dismantle and Heal

Blooming Tip

...As a result, somewhere between my late 20s and my early 30s, I developed cancer. I wasn't diagnosed with cancer, but I didn't need the diagnosis to know what was happening within my body. I literally felt the cancer cells multiplying within. I felt the residual pain in my chest, deeply within my vaginal walls, and throughout the sides of my body. My periods were extremely painful and heavy. Excess mucous formed in my body, so much so that most mornings I thought I had a cold. The way I was processing life was killing me and my body was reacting to the trauma I had placed upon it by mismanaging my emotions (energy in motion) for years. While all that was beautifully taught to me was taught with the best intentions, it didn't serve my best interest. I had to change how I was living and loving. I had to invite new thoughts into my body. I had to be responsible for my healing. I had to encounter something different from what I was taught; Mum had just made her transition after living 10 years with (diagnosed) cancer but lived through me ... **the more evolved me.** The evolved me learned to make love to nature, to focus on what I love (nature's collective, music, arts, intimacy, feminine wisdom, movement, travel, embodying love, and lovemaking), to exercise and tap my body for activation, to spend whole days in internal and external orgasm, to implement more nutrient-dense juices and locally sourced vegetables, and to explode into ecstasy at any moment without concern or worry.

Just 'glow' for it.

Make it happen.

Do that thing you've been wanting to do.

How it turns out is relative.

Whether it turns out good or bad depends on how you script it.

It's your experience.

Voice, Memory, And Activation: The Holy Trinity

I like your deep voice; I told you this all the time. In fact I was thinking of you on my walk home today from the tea spot we used to visit. I should have just called you, but the thought of you was such a private and intimate moment that I didn't even want to spoil the splendor of your memory since we no longer talked. *I wonder if that makes sense even to me.* Because sometimes, my mind wanders, and I can't solidify a thought or a moment in my mind that is not too heavy enough to hold onto. So no matter how I am feeling, I soften even more. Let go of tension and holding. And increase the physical sensations inside my body knowing that the thoughts will enter me. Regardless. And they will leave. Eventually. Like you. I like them have their way.

How lovely that one single thought activates a connection with someone because the physical body doesn't know the difference between the imagined and the actual experience taking place. I wonder when I think of your voice is it because you thought of mine first and synced that connection.

But for some reason, you came up more than once as a tangible thought. And I don't want to give those tangible 'tastes' up, because they don't happen for me all of the time.

And it was so real. The way that you moved inside me, the pressure of my deep insecurity hiding inside of you, and the strength of your intense grasp on my ass... oh the sound of your voice ... I can't get over your sound, because it really is interesting that someone like you connected to my world for so many, many moons. And you still manage a way to connect through these steaming thoughts. Yet —I don't know who you are though ... not every single day of course.. Because you'd changed like leaves of Fall, and while change is always delicious, too much change is like trying to boil a cracked egg. It doesn't all solidify—and comes out a bit mushy.

And somehow getting to know you was a revealing process. It was revealing not of you though, but of me. Because I'm not too sure what I've built you out to be, but I do understand my fear of you revealing your true self and me being either completely disappointed or completely wet with wild desire to just mount you upon sight (and sound). I don't want to be either, but it's pretty clear to me that there are only two directions for me to go. So I soften. And let the thoughts be. Then I.......... oh glory.

I guess my point is that I cannot be unaffected by you as I am by most. And I hadn't planned on meeting anyone new or reconnecting with old connects, not even within my streams of thoughts. Not anyone who could alter who I am, since on some level, I need to be exactly who I am right now. But you have already affected me.

*Ahhhh.....*I often believe that there is a reason why we exist in other people's lives, and not as independent entities, we kind of need each other even when we pretend we don't. We came out of a person because we are only human when connected with a woman in some capacity. So I made the choice to surrender to my desires. To meet women. Become lovers. And every person that I have around influences me in an evolutionary (and revolutionary) way, even if, sometimes, they aren't a complete positive contribution to my life. I feel their presence and it allows me to grow. And on some days, soar.

But with you well I'm not sure where you fit. I'm not clear on what your role is or why it is that you have (as I see it) walked into my life (again even if only within my memory). On a subtle level I must confess that I have used the "law of attraction" all of my life, and in that effect, I have always gotten what I wanted. I have always received what was asked. So I keep meeting you in these other worlds.

With you my main question is what are you the answer to? What have I asked for that you will provide? What is it that you need from me? I'm oh so curious to figure this out, because I give thanks for the opportunity to receive you. Even in the watery stream of one single memory.

But if you know, if you have an idea, or perhaps, if you are the one who has requested me, then tell me. I would love to hear it. I would love to know the question. And as I request it, I am sure you will tell it to me. Even if you are unaware, somehow I think that the question is hidden in the memory of your voice. Because I know your voice ... that Afro-German accented voice. Through your sound, the memory of your sound, the mere thought of you, I at least understand that, yes, you are the answer at least for right now in this second ..... that's what I do know for now. So I touch myself in reverence and praise of your sound. In celebration of that voice when it decides to show up inside me. And I do not feel shame. I just simply spread and spray the gift of vulnerability.

Blooming Tip

You don't have to fight anything.

Not exes,

jobs,

emotions,

experiences,

or injury and illness.

Simply love them in the deepest part of your soul into higher vibrations.

Doctors diagnosed my mum with breast cancer, but I knew she was transitioning in her body because of..... heartbreak. I remember when it happened, who the person was, and how it happened. I was about 12 years old. I wonder why doctors never ask patients how their hearts are doing. If their hearts are open, chip, or broken. Through that experience along with a few of my own personal experiences I learned that I had to own my joy, magic, and wonder so that no matter what a person does or doesn't do I still had some left inside. I had to marvel in it outside the context of money, relationships, degrees, and full time employment. When I released the 1st edition of "You Look Like Something Blooming" I remember being in a state of euphoria at an internet cafe after camping out on the Earth for nearly one month. I had no consideration for whether the book was perfect or if it would sell one single copy; I was simply in deep joy that I was doing what I love! I'm not like that always but what a celebration to have that magical moment stored in my subconscious mind--to know that I can be..when I choose to simply to be.

We live inside these vast enormous universes, or body temples, and there is deep value in being a human spirit who LIVES inside her/his/their body. You are not at the mercy of doctors or institutions, but if you must go to doctor, consider choosing one whose background is some brand of integrative medicine. With that consideration, learning how these little body vessels work on the subtle planes is beneficial for every area of your life. I was my mum's primary caregiver the last two years of her life and I used to fuss at those doctors, only to realize that they can only do what is within their sight or conscious understanding. They are entitled to their diagnoses and opinions and while they diagnosed her with breast cancer, *I could see how beneath the cancer was heartbreak, and that she in fact transitioned because of a broken heart (that never recovered).* How her heartbreak created an environment for cancer cells to rapidly replicate. How stress, unresolved harsh emotions, work/life imbalances, and lack of touch foster dis-ease in the body. This was in 2003. How perfect that the heart sits between the breasts.

41

IX

Consider not judging

your emotions as

positive or negative.

Consider them neutral

and delight in the opportunity

to live inside of them.

Only then will emotions

know that they are safe

to come,

flow,

and eventually transform.

 All emotions are valid and worthy.
Be gentle with them. They need
your support.

X

Anger is such an attention-grabbing powerful emotion when transformed into creative action.

Otherwise it stinks, rots the organs, and diseases the entire body temple.

How do you transform anger into creative action?

XI

Breast Leadership

She adores glazing her breasts
with sweet oils, raw honey, and moonlight.

Bathing her round coins in the belly of the sun and
Mississippi river water.

Activating her magic in ways that attract kind touch.

Lending them over to her lover
for nourishment and support.

Rubbing them in circles, activating their receptors.

Receiving information and fulfilling her dreams.

Allowing. her breasts. to lead her life.

No wonder they sit out in front... in service to her highest honor.

—

Breast-Blooming Tip

Make it a habit to massage your breasts daily, like brushing your teeth. When heightened activation is needed such as depression, massage them hourly. If you work outside of your home, go to the bathroom, massage them upwards and inwards towards your heart for one minute. Gently pinch your nipples and feel deeply into the arousal. As you massage your breasts, smile into them through your heart. Get your body acclimated to being aroused at work... anytime. Living inside this heightened state will simply make you a better employee, parent, partner/lover, sibling, or friend. *You are here for your pleasure before you are here for anything else.* Because only a *human* spirit who inhabits a body temple can experience tactile pleasure. Spirits who live in abandoned buildings or trees don't receive that luxury.

XII

MONEY/CHA-CHING

What we refer to as 'money' is simply energy, and how well we harness that energy is our source of abundance or lack.

Blooming Tip

Go back to your childhood: Can you remember the first things you heard about money? *'Money don't grow on trees'* is what I repeatedly heard to indicate that money was hard to access and therefore there was never enough.

To those words and subconscious mind programming I now say:

'Cancel, delete, and uncreate in all times, spaces, and dimensions.'

That's right! Whenever you say words, phrases, or statements, the energies inside those words, phrases, and statements begin to take roots into your subconscious mind. In order to stop the growth process, you will need to follow the words, phrases, or statements with a **verbal action** that neutralizes the **energy (growth process).** **Even though I was citing an example of my past programming, I still neutralized the thought about money and trees, because everything I and any person say WILL bloom in some way.**

BUT IN REALITY MONEY DOES GROW ON TREES (giggles)

Had I not neutralized what I said, those words would have taken root in my life and INTO my body—with no consideration that I was merely citing an example to write a book.

So you can either say, *'Cancel, delete, and uncreate in all time, spaces, and dimensions.'*

or

touch some earth and delightfully give the energy away to the earth (with pleasure).

Or simply say *'clear'* or whatever word feels deliciously clearing to you. Keep it simple....call it your "safe" word...mmm!

To undergo a deeper clearing, take a VERY cold shower!!!

Shock your body temple into clearing the seeds, roots, and subsequent growth.

Flowers in bloom. Every bit of energy we hear, smell, taste, touch, speak, or sense goes inside. Divine Penetration.

Divine Penetration

XIII

CONSCIOUS MIND

VS

SUBCONSCIOUS MIND

The conscious mind: A place where dreams and goals are initiated. The present moment mind space.

The subconscious mind: The place providing the blueprint for you to carry out your dreams and goals. The fuel pump that initiates action (love) or inaction (fear).

Blooming Tip

The condition of your body is a reflection of your subconscious mind.

Everything you learned, experienced, or witnessed from ages 0-8 years implanted itself into your subconscious mind and continues to inform and influence your life and experiences even as an adult.

To transform your life, you <u>must</u> go back into your childhood and rewrite (reshape) your stories, where EVERYTHING you experienced, witnessed, and observed between ages 0-8 years old holds the frequency of love and translates as a place of power and love in your cells, tissues, and organs.

Otherwise you stunt your capacity to transform your life.

Ask yourself: Are you still talking/experiencing/hearing the same messages you heard 2, 10, 20, 40, 240 years ago? Remember:

You are here in luscious heaven on earth to experience the senses, live a sensuous life, and evolve! *Even the messages you receive deserve to evolve.* Even "history" in all its magic, can evolve, especially in how it resonates in your mind and body. Munch deliriously on that!

Be brave enough to tinker with your subconscious programmings and create your very best life and love.

Learning how to connect with your animal totem is a Goddess tool to give insight, direction, support or resolve to pending issues, questions, or concerns. Dare yourself to notice nature. What animals do you sense most often? Sit inside your unique flow and harmony, and simply observe your way into the answer. The hardest part is TRULY taking out time to just sit, observe, and feel your way into nature's medicine.

XIV

BLOOMING TIP

Build an altar to your inner child.
Rewrite your childhood stories and
reprogram your subconscious mind

How to build an altar to your child self (inner child):

Similarly to how you would build an altar to a Goddess, Jesus Christ, or other deity, you intuit and create it. Listen closely to what your angels, guides, mystics, elementals, or any other holy energies are communicating with you. The major thing you want to consider is that this altar is for your inner child, so to invoke your inner child you will need to implement things on your altar that brings her/him/them out. What were your favorite snacks as a child? If you weren't vegan, please don't put vegan snacks on your altar! You want those M&Ms, chick-o-sticks, cotton candy, anything you ADORED as a child. If you have any childhood stuffed animals or other toys, place them on your altar. This sacred space should feel inviting to your inner child and should make that person smile.

Once you have built your altar to your inner child, you are ready to activate the energy around your NEW stories.

YAYY!

This is the gray part of the activation process: Activation of new stories is not a monolithic process. I know people will say there's one way to do this or that and provide instructions, but that's just simply isn't true. **I can give you a few seeds, but you will have to take those seeds and create your enchanting garden (the unique specialness that works for you). Ding, ding!**

One major thing I did was sat with my spirit and asked questions. Who am I? What did my other lifetimes look like? If you believe in lifetimes, you know that you are not limited to the experiences of this life to extract information from. Also I purchased a notebook, decorated it, and wrote my new stories in the contents. The answers to the question 'Who Am I?' live and continue to live within me and making time to sit at my altar enabled me to hear the answers.

Once you rewrite the old story, there is absolutely no reason to repeat the old story again. The old story is a myth, an illusion, a distortion of your higher self. You can be born again in this body. Start there. Now.

Here's a sacred piece of my story:

I have always been a very beautiful woman with each reincarnation. I was birthed into royalty each time, gold jewels, vines, and beads adorned my body minutes after being born. Two women influenced my activism in unconditional love, radical self care, nourishment, and pleasure. My mum and Aunt Gemma— we called her Gem for short. Mum helped me to unfold my activism therefore I always attracted anything I desired with EASE and timeliness. My aunt Gem— she taught me what a round ass and curvy body do for humanity. So I shape and cultivate my curves like ritual...

There's more to my story but I think you get the idea...

I have consistently chanted my mantra since 2006, at least 7—10 times per week. It lies prone in my subconscious mind- flowering into fruition—bit by bit. It takes me about 2 minutes to recite but now I do it from memory alone. One thing I can assure you is that you WILL see changes in your life, little affirmations that you hold command and dominion over your life, and that your desires have been met, you're merely catching up to them in your physical body. Get it?

I am now at a point in my life where anything I desire simply shows up. I point my pinky finger wand and it appears.

Rootworker

For a quick lift to your ass cheeks/an ass pick me up/stimulus to your root chakra: Have your ass cheeks massaged and deliciously played with by someone who stimulates your organs upon sight, sound, thought, or smell of said person......or try 25-50 reps of squats hourly. Deep breath and core (stomach) tight. Please don't extend your delicate knees over your toes. On the lift from the ground, smack your ass cheeks with both hands. Activate sound and allow a physiological reaction to come forward. I enjoy smiling or moaning or singing. Choose what works best for you depending upon the day.

XV

How often do you experience those things you love?

Sign your permission slip to experience what you love. You can experience anything you love inside the creative space of your mind. Your body doesn't know anything other than what the mind tells it. The more you experience it, the more you align your vibration to indeed attract the experience into your life. GET WILD, WET BETWEEN THE THIGHS, AND EXCITED IN YOUR MIND! THAT'S THE DRAW and FUEL YOU WILL NEED TO CREATE THE EXPERIENCE NOW. If not now, soon.

~Permission to experience what you love~

Blooming Tip

Consider becoming the type of energy that no matter where you go, where you are, you always add value to the spaces and lives of those around you.

XVI

In many cases, the US Big Pharmacy does NOT provide "medicine" for the human body, only chemicals that help to mask symptoms. This is not good or bad; it is what it is. Consider allowing love and deeper lovemaking, fresh fruits/vegetable juices, organic, hormone-free, animal products or wild meats in conjunction with an ENORMOUS amount of veggies, and herbs, plants, spirit, healing relationships & community, touch, the moon, trees, red clay soil, mama earth & full blown sunshine to be your medicine. *Be empowered to attract whatever prescription works best for your body temple.*

What are your current medicines? What can you do to implement more alternative medicines (i.e. sunshine) into your body temple?

These statements have not been evaluated by the FDA. Praise be.

"Expensive" organic foods NOW or exorbitant pharmaceutical drugs LATER?

You always have a choice.

XVII

Dare not shrink in your body simply because you are afraid to love again.

The condition of your body is a product of your thinking, particularly subconscious thought. Consider not spending ANY part of your life denying love, and subsequently denying your cells, tissues, and organs the capacity to come alive and serve their purposes. Literally your titties will shrink and deflate and your booty will turn inward, not wanting to be nourished, seen, or heard from. Keep up the enthusiasm, fire, and passion in favor of love. Burst yourself into a wet sea at the mere thought of love. The brilliancy is that the body is only receiving whatever the mind is TRULY believing.

BLOOMING TIP

A Goddess' bathroom may want to feel like her hydrotherapy room. Clean, naturally disinfected (vinegar + citrus (the juice or essential oils of lemon, lime, or orange squeezed into spray bottle/shake well & move your hips during the shake/refrigerate for later use/make only enough to last 10 days or less)), as chemical-free as possible, and organized. So many miracles and magic happen in the bathroom.

(An accidental portrait of my bathroom sink)

—

We learned who we were, what we were, and how we are
expected to behave but if we choose, we can deconstruct all that
we have learned about ourselves and the programs placed into
our subconscious minds, and create anew. It's our divine gift and choice to do so.

When we perceive differently, the world interacts with us differently.

XVIII CONFESSIONS: A STORY

"She spends whole days in uncontrollable ecstasy.

And no one is there but her and her higher self.

Alone time feels good going inside."

—India Ame'ye

Life showed up and processed differently for me when I realized that everything is sex and sexual. Once I learned that, life became dare I say easy or easier. It's like when you're watching a movie and begin to cry. You are being penetrated in your heart to trigger tears. Penetration is sexual; the movie scene is going inside you. Ahhh (throat open please). Sitting in nature is sexual. Communicating with a stranger is sexual, as the communication gives rise to the inner body penetration or what we call "feelings." Watching CNN is sexual; the news either leaves you frustrated, hopeless, or pissed off. The information has penetrated and is now inside the body. With that consideration and understanding, when I now eat food or drink something tasty, I send that excitement, nourishment, and joy throughout my entire body temple. I allow the penetration, allowing my yoni to be penetrated, allowing is usually difficult the part. But once I got over that hump, the healing in the organs happened ... sometimes generational; sometimes ancestral; sometimes neighborly; sometimes I don't have the language to express exactly what it was/is. You know that you are healing when you can love deeply, abundantly, unconditionally. When I'm allowing penetration, I breathe deeply in and out and move my breath throughout my body temple with my mind, utilizing my mind as a tool as oppose to allowing my mind to utilize me as a pawn.

XIX

She saunters into a crowded room
not as a victim of the world,
not full of shame,
not insecure,
not doubtful,
not limited,
not poor,
not broken,
not heavy in her heart.
Only light on her feet,
navigating her fears,
communicating through her spine
as the indomitable and juicy presence of love.
Intentional in her choices,
Intentional in her language,
Intentional in her thinking,
Intentional in her creations,
and mighty intentional in her strut.

—Love Strut

BLOOMING TIP

Reconjuring a story is medicine. Who are you? And what does that
person feel like when she walks into a room? Take a break right
now and visualize her.

XX

only you

and your accompanying thoughts,

beliefs,

perceptions,

actions,

and self-abuse

can make yourself sick

and attract disease.

not even doctors

are taught this type of

agency. And there is

no such thing as a

cancer gene.

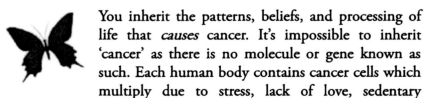

You inherit the patterns, beliefs, and processing of life that *causes* cancer. It's impossible to inherit 'cancer' as there is no molecule or gene known as such. Each human body contains cancer cells which multiply due to stress, lack of love, sedentary lifestyles, mismanagement of emotions, or past life necessities. Which begets the questions, 'is illness really a 'bad' thing" or 'is there such a thing a bad/good,' or 'is life simply about loving what is?'

XXI

Blooming Tip

Play footsies with the energy of life. Play with it, like a lover. Let this energy blow on your neck, kiss your face, massage your back, fondle your breasts, play with your anus, lift your thighs, and expose your fragrant flower. Let this energy remind you of your thesis and purpose in life: *to simply bloom.*

 Deconstruct. Reconstruct.

Everything works better in our bodies when we learn to simply adore ourselves, our pain, sadness, insecurities, and challenges included. Where there is no resistance or rejection, there can only be divine love. How sexy is that brand of healing?!

I dare you to let go of your accumulations and start a new thought, a new love, and a new life. And so I did.

ANEW: conversations with the Self Igniting Inspired Action

—

"I see my body as sci-fiction, an otherworldly entity with mostly non-human attributes, a creature with a human heart, that can shapeshift (change shapes) and morph into whatever it is I need and desire at any time. And so it happens...."-India Ame'ye

Activation Exercises to Bring Life Into Breast Tissue

You have breasts, ok, but it doesn't mean that you have life force magnetism inside your breast tissues. Below are some ways to help activate dull, life-less powerlines to the divine. As with all herbs, please consult your physician.

—

One. Consider incorporating fennel seed, fenugreek, maca, and cayenne pepper in any smoothie concoction or raw dish. Start off with a teaspoon per day and gradually increase to two teaspoons. Observe how your breasts respond. Do did feel firmer, fuller, more alive than before? Of course intake lots of water—use your intuition—feel your way into what makes sense for you. I drink about ¾ gallon per day. How about you?

Two. Self-massage your breasts or have your lover to engage your powerlines in touch and words of affirmation. Remember every part of the body is alive and needs to be held and adored.

Three. Have your breasts sucked more often by friend, lover, or even you. While your breasts are being kissed and sucked, imagine your lover's spit as nectar dropping into your heart, cleansing and healing it. Now when you walk, imagine the nectar flowing out of your feet and into your life and the lives of those you encounter. For Goddesses, rudimentary experiences evolve into magical, healing initiations.

If you could feel this current flowing through me. It's the same current flowing through the trees, rivers, soils, birds, deer, stars, and interplanetary whole. It's the same current that turns the body on.

XXII

I am no longer willing to place my own perceptions of what's 'right' or 'wrong' onto others, because what I perceive as 'right' or 'wrong' is ONLY 'right' or 'wrong' for me. My body spends less time trying to heal from the ache of someone not doing something I believe is 'right' or 'good' and can relax into *unconditional acceptance for all.*

One of best ways to ease discomfort in the body temple is being aware of when you are judging. You can say "cancel, delete, and uncreate" or any other set of words that satisfy your yum and make more space for others to be free from the burdens of judgment. As you make more space, the universe supports your own personal brand of freedom and offers you the same.

When someone believes that they can inherit a disease like heart disease, what they are saying is that they will inherit the biological programming that results in disease. Two different things.

Blooming Tip

My emphasis has always been on the energetics, the awakening, the release, the ecstasy and the joy that can be sip in any single moment. And the stillness, the ability to be able to become DEEPLY quiet, like a doorway into divine bliss and a healthy resting heartbeat. The ability not to lose the moment in lieu of past recitations and future projections. I would say it's my medicine to do my best not to miss too many creative moments. And to NOT just merely experience love but to embody the love in my cells, tissues, and organs. *Oh how the cure for cancer could live in one's capacity to simply allow more love inside on the in-breath.*

XXIII

My capacity to feel is what allows me to walk the earth typically in full blown arousal. But that arousal rarely has anything to do with another person or sex, more so my natural state of being. Another person simply adds to what already is. It makes me a lil bit 'giddy' sometimes to live out loud this way, but I am so attracted to my own brand of freedom.

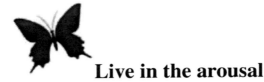 **Live in the arousal**

XXIV

If you are taking vitamin supplements on top of blockages inside your body temple, you may find that you are not getting results or results are fleeting and far between. Consider saving your money, quitting your supplements, and clearing the blockages first. Itemize the blockages in your pussy or breasts or throat or pinky toe. Where does it hurt ... then go deeper?! Get out bare into nature. Drink more fresh juices. Take an air bath or a milk bath. Sage your hair follicles. Cry- Scream- Write. Get Wild and creative so that supplements will have open pathways to do their work.

 Clarity before vitamins

BLOOMING TIP

You have to be ready
when your soul incarnates
into a brown body.
Don't get drained
from perplexed stares
and curious desires.
It's all that medicine
you hold between
your nourishing thighs
and brown eyes.
Don't shrink or feel shame
and poison the potion.
Strengthen your spine
and sweeten the Atlantic Ocean.

—Medicine women

When you walk as beauty, you heal and make way for
other generations to do the same. Your blood and bones
belong to the collective (including ancestors and future
babies), therefore your healing is the collective's healing.
Your healing is EVERYONE'S Healing.

~There's only one womb~

Godly intentions in some way, by some brand of smoke and ecstasy, turn into godly acts.

XXV

If you work for others,
be sure to make sacred space
to come into your wildness and magic at home.
Emerge out of dress codes and time clocks
and rules and regulations
into universal laws, warm salt water baths, ankle bells, and swinging breasts.
Devour fruit
as symbolism of future manifestations.
Don't be denied
and don't ever forget
that taking time to cultivate pleasure
and prosperity
offers more access to wealth than a 9 to 5.

Some of you have High standards because it's within your DNA; Royalty runs through your blood. You adore certain fabrics, stones, or high-vibrational foods like local honey, organic vegetables, or even cucumber water sipped out of a young coconut. You presently mimic your unconscious past. Beloved you are not wrong, the illusion that all things are not connected is what's wrong. Bask in the awakening!

"Glowing" through some challenges? Feeling disconnected from your body? Drained? Emotional? Try fasting on lemon and cucumber water between ¾ gallon -gallon per day, along with herbal tea concoctions such as burdock, ginger, cayenne, and vegetables juice. Dance in sunlight and moonlight. Sing. Slap your ass and hips to invoke activation...you probably know the deal by now. Do this for at least 3-5 days in a row. *You are truly glowing now!*

XXVI

I challenge myself not to see myself separate from whatever is taking place in life because separating myself leaves me helpless in my ability to produce real-live transformation and change, as I cannot truly expect to transform anything outside of myself. I can only transform what exists within me, as me. The strength of the human mind lives in the magic each one of us are connected to: **the collective consciousness**. As participators in the collective consciousness we are responsible for all things that happen to us. Even something as silly as my coworker acting like an ass means that I own responsibility in the creative process of said coworker's asinine behavior. So I act as if there in only one person in the situation—ME and change everything around me, in my environment, **through** changing a similar aspect that lives within me that my co-worker's behavior is merely highlighting for me to see where my work lies. How cute, we are all really ONE!

Whatever's inside pollenates everything
around you to bloom ... or not. And whatever pollenates through
the lens of your perception, pollenates inside your womb.

~Bee Pollen~

XXVII

BLOOMING TIP

INFUSE INTENTIONS INTO YOUR TEAS

My personal favorite cleansing tea: 1 tsp of all herbs in quart glass jar. Steeped 3-5 minutes. Let stand. Also consider not boiling your tea and pouring them directly into glass jar and leaving outside under the moon.

Burdock root, red clover, dandelion, a dash cinnamon, cayenne, and RAW LOCAL honey to taste
(for cleansing organs)

The results for me are clear skin, healthy digestion, and a balances in my body's PH.

...Delight in the opportunity to be your own doctor and do your own research.

Owning contentment for what stands before me eliminates internal suffering that I should be somewhere I am not.

Dare to utilize the power of a really good healing wand penis (you get to decide what that means for you) and allow the healing wand to utilize the power within you.

This feeling. Ferocious, swollen, and raw. Unceasingly vigorous and explosive. Barefoot and all-natural. Wet. A nourishing, knife-sharp necessity for one single moment. Feral in hormones and pheromones. Feral in water and fire. Feral in spirit and spit. Feral in sweat and sweetness. Feral in depth and mystery. Feral in smoke and ecstasy. Don't bring your illusive, learned constructions of safety. Don't bring an unbalanced ego and lack of freedom. Don't bring one single limitation on love. Bring your pure innocence, pure passion, the warm sun on your naked body. Bring your primal allegiance to softness and moisture. Bring your hunger for mystery and these thick thighs. I want to see you drink from the clearest hot spring. Bend me over until there's nothing left but crusts of mud underneath my fingernails. Paws and purrs. Slippin', slidin,' and motor-boatin' into the next in-breath. Cosmically ordained to immerse ourselves into one another's afterglow. Someday.

I love when women or feminine-embodied beings own that we make our lovers healthier and wealthier simply by being harmony with our feminine power and magnetism. After being with an empowered feminine being, lovers become a magnet to their goals and dreams. Simply put they become far more successful after being inside our grandest mystery. Sauntering when we walk, nourishing that pot of gold that lives within our asses, our 1st chakras, the root of all things magical, 'your majesty is here to serve.'

Sex is not a theatrical performance, educational lesson, or entertainment. Sex, when connected to the heart, ignites our divine most magical selves. A supreme connection to our body temples as healers. To share ourselves, to entangle ourselves in rapture, is to share the medicine stored inside our bodies. There's no pressure to perform, no need to 'beat it up' or 'make it clap' -- there's only the disillusion of time and space to be free. Open. Carefree. Undernourished in ego. Warm by light. Safe enough to orgasm in 3 minutes or 3 hours. Tap into the language of the womb. It cries out in pain. It speaks in tongues. It guides. It reacts to apologies. It whispers information. It contains a living library and the accompanying archives. It remembers all things. It is our mystery and deepest truth. It connects us to The Great Mother. The Earth.

Just remember that there's only one womb.

XXVIII

BLOOMING TIP

Take delicious responsibility for your life and all your past lives to invoke your power to create and manifest.

Someone sent me a message asking why I am no longer a feminist. That is a long essay to write, but the abridged version is that I find much of feminism reinforces the victimhood belief system that was deeply welded in my DNA. Victimhood is the antithesis of self-love and abundance! For many years I believed that someone could make me sad, or angry, or happy, not realizing that all those emotions were choices I beautifully unearthed within me based upon how I learned to react to what others were doing. I had no idea I could stop folks from breaking into my car by merely believing that no one would desire to break into my car. That I, in all my holy-ness, was 100% percent safe with the power of my command for safety in my anus (root chakra/life support center). Also I learned to shame and blame everything and everyone around me, as if I was not the creator of my experiences in my current and past lives, where someone was or is always doing something harmful to me without me having any agency over what happened. **My reality knows I create everything; there is no other person but me as everyone is a mirrored reflection in small and large ways.** And no this is not new-ageism, *it is indeed the metaphysics behind energy, attraction, magnetism, physics, chemistry, mathematics, and ancient African religion or African Traditional Religion, the blood that connects us ALL.*

And guess what, sometimes the most painful experiences were necessary for my growth and consequently the growth of the collective consciousness. I know that may be difficult for many to read and receive, but understanding some aspects of metaphysics changes you. You learn to release victimization and take full ownership of your life and ALL of your creations. With that, 100% self-responsibility becomes a magic tool of empowerment and ultimately transformation. When the source of everything in your life undoubtedly shifts to love, the world interacts with you differently. Certainly womanism has been a powerful tool for my healing and spirituality, and I would not be where I am today without those tools and learnings. I think the greater idea is that I am not deadlocked into anything that puts limitations on who I AM and my infinite ability TO CREATE, which means I relate to ALL through the abundant lens of love. I am the creator of ALL.

I ultimately realize that I am one with all things, and from this advantage point I can produce change and transformation in my life. I can transform my DNA, attract more abundance, heal my organs, shift my body type, heal a past life, and climax from wind. you name it . . . A shift in me is a shift in all. *Do you know how many lifetimes are inside just one pussyhole?* Oh please start your count there if you like. ♥

Lifetimes

XXVIII-Heart-pussy connection

TENDING TO YOUR HEART

is unfettered nourishment for your pussy.

Your heart and pussy are one in the same.

Therefore whatever happens to your heart

brilliantly translates in your pussy.

Wearing strings, charms, loops, circular objects, waistbeads or body chains instantly makes your waist smaller. I'm not even considering physically, I mean metaphysically. There's a metaphysical component to any and all things physical that informs a healthy body among many many other things. My focuses always begin there first.

XXX

Definition of love: The capacity to honor, respect, adore, and appreciate another human being or energy without ANY conditions or expectations. The moment a person places conditions and expectations onto another person or energy, s/he has stopped loving. Love is a total body and spirit abundance and the greatest holy ghost possession, where everything a loving person touches and interacts with turns into more love.

As an abundant and limitless spirit, it only makes sense to love abundantly. *Love is the richest form of expression and ecstasy any person can embody or encounter.* If your body is dominant in unresolved pain, unresolved illness (yes there is a resolve to illness), unresolved emotions that leave you stressed and restless, you will have an abundance of pain, illness, and distress to share with others until you sip your resolve. But if you embody love, if your body embodies love, you will want to share that love because essentially you can only share that which you possess. When possessed by the holy spirit of love, you may find yourself wanting to love more than person and sometimes, maybe even intimately share a bond and deeper connection with more than one. Just like you could never love just one baby, you should not be under some mandate to only love one person, whether there is intimacy is irrelevant. With love, pure love, there is never any lack or restrictions, only greater abundance of itself. I make love to different aspects of nature ... daily, feel me?! What if a tree had human attributes, becoming upset if I decided to love and embrace rain? How limiting would that be if I was unable to receive the gifts that rain had to offer my body temple, gifts that trees were not able to give me, because well, they're trees. —Silly, eh?!

The inner and outer transformation happened when I allowed myself to dig deeper into my experiences and resolve everything back to love. Every way that I am is divine; my experiences are all divine and I am incapable of encountering an experience that is not divine. With that, **I do love and appreciate monogamy**, the opportunity to intimately connect my glorious body temple with another person and direct intentions, spells, and incantations into us ... in the wildest and most uninhibited ways ... love that! However that doesn't mean any other form of intimacy with another person should NEVER be considered ... it's really kinda silly when you think about it. I am NOT talking about going to some club and TRYING to hook up or meet folks for sex ... none of that. I am talking about the choice to honor relationships when there is a genuine natural attraction or pull towards another person and you may want to explore it ... or maybe not. That part is really irrelevant. It's more relevant that a loving conversation can be held about your and/or your partner's attractions to others without you, your spouse, partner, or lover walking away feeling unloved simply because the other is feeling activated and alive in her/his body temple enough to simply feel ... the sweet feeling of attraction. Nothing inherently wrong with having attractions to others, it's when we are not allowed space to be authentic that we heat up our fallopian tubes and create internal distress and illness in our body temple as a result.

Blooming Tip

What I know is that at the end of day, I trust my lover, the person I sleep with as I trust myself ... with pleasure! If I love ... then that means I trust. Without concern or conditions. Period. And that's all I know. **If I am TRULY loving that means am simply trusting.** _____

Beloved, don't throw yourself to the lions this time around; just bring your tired self to me. Bring the spoilages of war and the pain you wear and plate it at my decorated feet. Bring the horses, lamb, and jewels from the Kingdom you defeated. Offerings of snake skin, glass jars of honey, and the farmland you reaped. Allow me to massage away the contracts of depression from old childhood wounds. To slowly remove my dress and display the Chocolate you yearned for while away. Unearth the soft mounds of pointed earth and the river and trees running along my curved spine. Oh do your holy dance, your sacred warrior call and response. <u>But forget about gender for a moment</u>. Study Ogun and Shango, then embody the masculine fire by bringing that sacred energy into your royal honor. Soon enough we revolve around one another like the moon and sun and sacredly suck our way into lifetimes of transformations, spraying and playing, waxing and waning, where everything and every experience is resolved back to love and loving. This incarnation doesn't have to be a war too. This time you have options.

~Beloved, this incarnation doesn't have to be a war ~

XXXI *"SOMETIMES YOUR VERY PRESENCE CAN SERVE AS NOURISHMENT FOR OTHERS." -INDIA AME'YE*

I.

While I agree it's a layered, complicated world, I also understand that the world is a projection, a collective projection—perhaps, but definitely a projection I participate in and influence through my beliefs, ruminations, creations, and experiences. My conscious and certainly SUBCONSCIOUS beliefs are either *medicinal or poison* —and do influence how life interacts with me. Period. My perceptions about life ripple out into the world and bring harmony and love or disharmony and disease, even in places (seemingly) as far as Nigeria.

Sure I could *google* the horrible sex trafficking crimes in other places, harp on how "bad" the world is, and talk about the pain and discomfort until I have nearly eaten away all of my cells tissues and organs, or march on Washington until my hips split. I can do this ... and for those who choose to do those things—**gratitude** for your choices. But I can also go into my inner world and experience my little life here in Georgia as a source of my activism—where, wherever I go, I not only share love but also bring MORE love and harmony into the environment, and that love and connection reach everyone bit by bit, including those in Nigeria and other faraway places! An aside: Sincerest gratitude to those who have marched and protested and to those who will.

Our face-to -face interactions with others can become real LIVE healing experiences that generate more love, where even the ordinary blooms into the extraordinary, where theories and dogma are actually put into practice.

What we give life is received by the moon and shines into all of us while we rest.

II.

If you believe that we are all connected, perhaps you can see how something as simple as cooking and sharing a meal with someone you love in NYC can also promote varying degrees of transformation and change, even in spaces as far as Nigeria. How YOUR genuine loving and compassion for those around you become transformative and healing cross continents. How everything you do is always much LARGER than YOU!

 **-Acts I and II**

Blooming Tip

Consider allowing your living and loving to be sources of your activism.

I am completely present to the absence of tension, worry, or anxiety about anyone or anything in this divine moment."— Navel Chakra Affirmation (For releasing butterflies in the belly)

XXXII

Consider not judging

your emotions as

positive or negative.

Consider them neutral

and delight in the opportunity

to live inside of them.

Only then will emotions

know that they are safe

to come,

flow,

and eventually transform.

 All emotions are valid and worthy. Be gentle with them. They need your support.

XXXIII

A lot of women (and men) have altars without even knowing it. They collect rocks or stones, feathers, seashells, candles, photos, water, essences, and so on and place them strategically around the houses or in their cars. And when they look at their collection, they feel the warmth of pleasant memories. I realized something as I moved about the US, traveling the land ... not quite able to have a traditional altar set up and not wanting to create a traveling altar. My body temple is my altar. I give it daily offerings. I even drink water out of glass instead of plastic bottles. I decorate my body with hearts and butterflies and chains and seashells. I love to pray over various parts of my body, like my heart, liver, and skin. Most days, when I look at it, I feel pleasant, soft, and warm feelings. It's rarely a sexual feeling (sexual feelings are wonderful), but it's not what I feel. I feel a deep sense of nourishment, that I have given my spirit (and body) space to love, experience, and transform.

I am witnessing the intentional magic in choosing what I want in life and trusting the process that leads me there. It's my place to retreat, inside my self, into the watery mystery, the only place that blooms femininity (and evolved masculinity), as each human body is a mix-bag of both polarities. It's my place to make inner adjustments to accommodate my outer visions. It's a cleanse and clearing in the deepest sense. I get away only to sit at my altar. To sit inside my Self.

 **Living Altar for Serpent Woman**

XXXIV

Be like a flower ... sometimes.

Where ever you are, you are the sweetest spot on Earth...

A subject of beauty

emitting the fragrance of love

with squishy thighs and a beating heart.

A flower shopping for groceries

or walking in a grassy knoll,

easily excitable and deeply pleasurable to encounter.

—Full Bloom

Sometimes

wake

up

and

do

nothing

but

take care

of

your womb.

XXXV

Two people experience the exact same event but are impacted in radically different ways.

Perception is always The Holy Goddess.

How you perceive is what you receive, not just into your mind but into your cells, tissues, organs, and your whole entire existence.

Perception is the Holy Goddess

BLOOMING TIP

The prime purpose of many jobs is to numb employees away from *feeling* and into monolith thought and fear-based programmings. You pretty much lose your *whole* self, but *seemingly* gain only microscopic bits of the company.

To not be able to feel anything outside of your work, only do what is expected and mismanage the accompanying stress without any consideration for what you need for your harmony and nourishment.

And it's **not** the company's issue because you are the one holding the imprint and choices.

Consider attracting pleasurable ways to experience your creativity in your workplace.

If you can find ways to be inside your pleasure more often than not, you win!

Consider wearing yoni eggs, your *best* lace panties, and waistbeads. Dress up from the inside out.

<u>Taking time</u> to feed fresh juice to your cells *dresses* up your inner
body which enhances your magic and magnetism for success in
your outer body.
Become involved in creative hobbies.
Don't be afraid to ignite your imagination and daydream.
To win while working
is far more valuable than any dollar amount you will ever receive.
To win while working is *invaluable life support and sustainable
living in practice.*

Blooming Tip

*Abundance is the ability to burst into a wet sea
and the mere thought of love and loving.*

 Can you imagine the total body bliss
encountered at the MERE thought of
love? Can you imagine what would
happen when that repeated thought send
signals out into the universe to ignite the actual, tangible
experience?

That's the power and brilliancy behind one single
thought.

What are you thinking about right now?

If it is within your harmony, write it here:

_____

_____

XXXVI

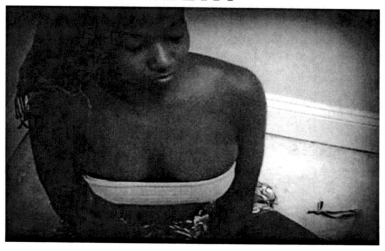

Sadness showed up at my celebration party.
Dressed in her black fishnet bodysuit and hooker
boots. The bitch gets on my nerves sometimes!

No RSVP. No phone call. Totally unannounced.

Just glowing, like the full moon in Gemini. Pretty as she could be. I invited her inside my home, a place I affectionately call 'The Godis Temple.' An ancient and sacred space that houses my centuries old soul. A complex soul that remembers my mornings bathing in milk and honey and afternoons dancing naked under full blown sunshine with my titties hanging out like ripe fruit. Looking like I was ready to be fertilized every way I turned.

I offered Sadness the option of fresh juice or wine. I told her she always had a choice in what she desired. She chose the juice and said she'd have the wine later, a subtle indication that she was planning to stay longer than I expected.

She joined in on my goddamn celebration party. Started furiously dancing like it gave her some type of room to breathe. To let go and surrender. She swirled the midnight into morning, never seeming to notice me watching her ass move. She had a grind like you wouldn't believe ... one of those natural, down-home, southern girl grinds. All three of my eyes tranced out on her wild, untamed sensibilities. I was in love.

Then suddenly like the wind in March, she left. Before I could thank her for showing up, Sadness was gone ... just like that. I knew we spoke the same cosmic language so I sent her a message of gratitude within my mind. I told her she had the right to be here too, that she was just as valuable as happiness.

Blooming Tip

Cry.
Moan.
Scream.
Laugh.
Yodel.
Sing to the sky.
Curse (conjure verbally).
Eat blueberries or blue potatoes or drink blue martinis.
Ask the earth for permission to wear blue flowers or lapis.
Speak clearly.
Suck her,
suck him,
or a cucumber or papaya or both
slooooowly
with your eyes open.
Because sexual frustrations and shame are stored in the throat chakra.

 ## Ways to clear and liberate your voice, speech, and communication

XXXVII

How brilliant is it that you are doing everything to yourself?! Think about that for a minute. If you can receive that into your organs, now you the capacity to undo anything that's been done, since **all history lies in the organs**. Because if other people are indeed doing things to you: hurting you, mistreating you, being mean to you, taking advantage of you, cheating on you, without your influence in the creation, then you eliminate your opportunity to change and transform those experiences. Because how can anyone change anything outside of themselves. Get it?

Healing Transformation

We learn to be insecure about the very things that heal us: attraction, beauty, connection, love, and the like, but life is beautiful and people show up to grow us, adore us, love us—and most of us need it! Deeply! Life is pretty complex sometimes, but the reality is it isn't very complex when relearn how to love—and what that word means in the most abundant sense. I helped make Mum and Dad's lives easier, and they helped to do the same for me financially—and certainly we could have all loved one another if allowed. The more representations of love a child has in her/his/their life, the more value that's seeded within the child, and the easier life is for all parties involved.

Blooming Tip

The human body is most programmable during the first 30 minutes after waking up and final 30 minutes before going to asleep. Here lies the opportune times to recite goals and dreams and most importantly *let them enter your anus (root chakra) and make you smile. The consciousness of dreaming helps to foster transformation in your life.*

Sweet dreams and Good Moaning!

When on your moon, eat bloody red foods and activate your unique lunar energies. There's so much value in the human body, all you have to do is remember.....

XXXVIII

Consider not just creating a vision board, but **breathing life** into the vision board through your emotion. Let the vision board get you enormously wet between the thighs and butt cheeks. Produce sweat under your underarms when you greet your vision board for the day. Don't just build a vision board and tack it to a bare wall. Intentionally place it somewhere where it can receive charges, near plants, in nature, or close to your altar. Otherwise it's just pictures on cardboard.

 Vision boards need life force in order to activate. How can you make your vision board come alive?

What do you want from me? You want to bend me over, stick your tongue inside my tight spaces? Taste the clarity and light dripping from my pussy? Squeeze my quarter-sized nipples? Or do you just want to go on this date? What is it you really want from me?

The Mindful Whore and the Priestess have always been ONE.

XXXVIII

REPROGRAMMING THROUGH REVISIONING

After 15 years of dating/intimately loving/sharing my body temple/engaging relationships with women only, I reconnected with beautiful and brilliant men again alongside my forever love for women.

I never set out to reconnect with men again. I was a self-identified lesbian and very proud.

But revisioning my past was alchemy, deconstructing my beliefs, walls, and every illusions that I had ever encountered.

Revisioning my past opened my heart to the deepest form of healing.

Revisioning my past channeled love into ALL my past experiences.

Revisioning my past allowed me to forgive others, only to realize there was never, ever anyone to forgive. As a living Goddess, I twirled in the power that taking ownership of my life produced in my life.

Revisioning my past bloomed abundance and greater possibilities. Abundance simply means more choices.

Revisioning my past became a tool of transformation in area of my life. I came to realize that I have choices that included male lovers and could also embrace masculine energy through a delicious penis (healing wand) that belonged to what is socially perceived as a biological male. OH YUM! Sucking on a healing wand that belonged to a body that I was emotionally connected to within complete trust and Godlike thrusts sent my orgasms into other dimensions where I could extract information to guide and heal my body in this dimension.

And so it is.

When transformation comes you never really know what it will look like, but one thing for sure you can count on:

You will close your eyes, whirl around, and when you open your eyes again, life will appear differently.

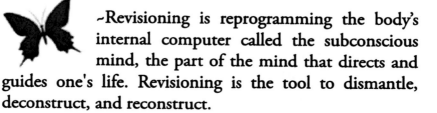 ~Revisioning is reprogramming the body's internal computer called the subconscious mind, the part of the mind that directs and guides one's life. Revisioning is the tool to dismantle, deconstruct, and reconstruct.

How I (revisioned) reprogrammed my past

I created a daily mantra and spoke it out loud with what the elders called 'wordsoundpower' meaning with force and great pride, alongside the generous assistance of my ancestors, the blood that runs through my body. I also utilized nature's hand and ear. I walked miles into nature and chanted:

*"I have always been a very beautiful woman with each creation.
I was birthed into royalty each time-gold jewels, vines, and beads adorned my body minutes after being born..."*

It kinda sounded like I was talking about Jesus.

But that's the point.

When you reprogram through revisioning, you can be anything you want to be-including Jesus. Sounds wild—Perfect!

Wait until you read the rest of this book!

The most important thing to remember is when you recite your mantra, FEEL each word inside your body temple. Let these words fill the space up inside your emotions. Get excited, silly, horny, or angry (if anger is your go-to emotion), allow yourself simply to feel the vastness of everything. The FEELING is the ENERGY you need to SUMMON in the reprogramming. You create the vision of WHO YOU ARE (NOT WHAT YOU WERE TOLD) and reprogram your past with your recitations.

You and all your lusciousness hold the alchemical processes to incite change. One of the less internally exhausting and cellularly-damaging ways to change anything is to see yourself as a part of the very thing you wish to change. This is the nature of spirituality, metaphysics, science, nature, ancient religion, mathematics, medicine, and energy in how it moves and operates. In deeper ways, it is near-impossible to change anything that isn't part and parcel of you; it is you in all your divinity who holds the chemistry, molecules, DNA, life force, sacred geometry, love, and creativity and all the ways it expresses itself to effectively produce deep layers of change and transformation. At any moment, it is you who has the unshakeable capacity to choose love and loving.....I am reminded...and I am remembering over and over again . It is far more beneficial to just touch people, share with people, love people, and I really mean love--not to be confused with possession..and keep all things just that simple.

XXXIX

Worry is nothing more than faith in an undesired outcome. It is just misuse of your miracle creating power of imagination. In fact the universe is neutral to your thought, decision and action. So whatever vibes you deliver to universe, you will attract as your reality——eventually. It's the nature of energy, physiology, mathematics, science, or spirituality. I am learning not to misdirect my faith and hold on to my desires; my body has less work to do to, only to remain at ease, inside the stillness of one transformative moment.

XL

Sex is an intense, communicative merging between the organs of two or more people, requiring little to no movement to reach ecstasy, nirvana, or healing. When you know the depth of what is REALLY taking place on the physiological and spiritual levels, you can select a delicious and worthy partner (or partners) accordingly. --Merging (Organ)isms/Penetrative Beings

---

Alkalizing the body with highly nutritious foods, thoughts, deeds, and love is the path to enjoying condom-free sexual intercourse and connection without worry, concern, or any other types of fear or painful outcomes. There is NO dis-ease, illness, or regret that can possibly attract and therefore penetrate ANY form of light and love. Think about it. You are not a victim nor are you on stand-by for destruction. It is because your spirit —in conjunction with your body —holds every ounce of the power! It is also because intercourse without a condom is the Holy Grail!

Condom-free sex when combined with your sense of power~

An aside: If you feel fear when sexually connected with another, that's OK. It's a signal that you probably shouldn't have sex with this person, as gorgeous as said person is. <u>If you do feel fear and still desire to have sex with the person, that's ok too.</u> If penis and vagina penetration is involved, please consider using a condom.

XLI

your spirit could give a fuck about money
when it's time to go,
spirit disrupts everything around you,
until you grow wings
and fly to your next destination,
landing magically and sometimes clumsily on your feet.
somehow still standing. And ready!

Bird women: Jobs and relationships

XLII

you don't ever

want to get in some

learned mindset that keeps

you from opening your heart.

~the space inhabiting love is the same energetic space that heals

---

Blooming Tip

You don't have to be perfect when doing THIS healing work (or anything else for the matter), it's making the effort to do something different, something that makes you uncomfortable, that sparks bits and pieces of your radical transformation. Don't get discouraged. Your learning is your nourishment.

Say this out loud!!
"I smell of love.
I taste of love.
I moan as love.
My hips move to the beat of love.
AND I am only capable of being entered by love."
—The Heart's Invocation: (The heart's translation in the pussy| Sacral/heart chakra connection.|The heart and pussy are ONE!

XLIII—BREAST MASTERY AND ACTIVATION (SENSORIAL TUTORIAL)

Below are steps to bringing LIFE into your breasts outside of getting pregnant and producing breast milk or having them sacredly sucked by someone you have a HEART connection with. <---Both experiences activate breasts, but there's more to learn and love. OH YAY!

I. Clear the armor around your heart by thinking of any visual that brings a smile to your face. Even if you have to sit for a few minutes, visualize a tasty, sweet, kind, loving, or silly moment. The smile means that you are present, available to your body, and awakened within your heart in this moment.

II. Clasp the palms of your hands together! POP! Hear the sound (the clap) of your hands coming together. Rub your palms together as fast as you can. Feel the HEAT (Fire!) being generated by your hand movements. The fire generated is the impetus to your breast activation and transformation. Think about how fire deconstructs and destroys the old and forges a way for something *new*. Thank you to old, and welcome to new. Transformation keeps us juicy!

III. With your fiery hands, massage your breasts in circular motions upwards and inwards, if you desire fullness and firmness. Outwards and downwards for reduction and firmness. Relate to the sensorial tutorial as you relate to your own body. Feel the movement within your own body. And flow with your unique harmony. *I trust you!*

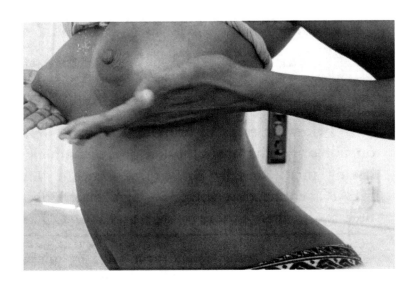

I started applying sea salt to my breasts after discovering that some older African women gently applied salt to their breasts to tighten their skin's pores and strengthen the elasticity. Sounds tasty to me!! When I thought about salt, I remembered how salt had been used to cast away unwanted spiritual entities and energies, so I utilize salt to assist me in clearing and opening my heart as well. If I have been brilliantly taxed emotionally (stressed!), I lightly wet my entire body and cover it in Himalayan sea salt. I allow the salt sit on my skin for 30 minutes before washing it off in cool water. I gush over how the salt reduces that size of my pores so that I don't get pimples on my *power lines to the divine.* I also massage the salt into my skin and allow it do work its magic while topless in the sun. Of course the salt eventually falls off, but the harmony that happens within my breast tissue is truly medicinal, particularly

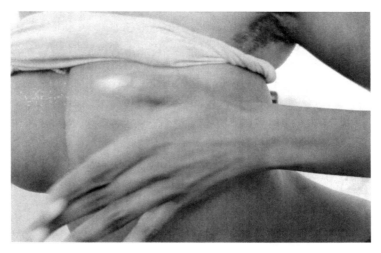

with the heightened sensitivity, activation, and magnetism (yes breasts attract if it's within the harmony of the woman to enable them to be magnetic. No more harsh talk about your body parts either!! Remember that your body is alive and your wishes (by way of your thoughts and self-talk) are surely its command! I consider this sacred Goddess work: the clearing of energies and the renewal of life inside the breast tissue. It's Goddess work to *take the time* to even do so.

XLIV

When joy resides in the organs, anything can be transmuted.

Organ health is essential for the healing of the body temple. Visualize joy—don't make it too hard. Just imagine a moment where you felt pure joy or visualize a joyous moment that you will experience in the future. Feel penetrated by joy. The joyous penetration means that the information is inside your body. Be guttural; make animal sounds! Unearth the wetness in your mouth portal. Expose your throat so dearly enthralled over your joy! Of course, as always, let this joy make you smile. The most optimal times are right before you fall asleep and first thing in the morning. Remember you are the closest to accessing spirit during these opportune times.

Blooming Tip

When the body has been used for love, health and abundance are inevitable!

XLV -
"Embodying self-responsibility is less about self-blame, and more about the ongoing ceremony and celebration of our divinity as creators, like look at me, 'I'm such a Goddess I created that, now let me create something differently''--I say that all the time actually." India Ame'ye

They (essentially.... "they" is you integrated in the collective) tell
you to be afraid. To follow the media. To stop feeling and trust
newspaper headlines. Give your emotions over to reporters.
You listen long enough to lose your powers,
become ill,
and usher in death transformation.

You're born again ... only to remember that...

What you focus on becomes your reality.

Then you channel the courage to go deep into the bone marrow,
pull out the pain
and
live transformation out loud
and on purpose.
You fortify radical paradigm shifts
in blood,
and actualize dreams
in organs.
You heal generations
with climaxes
and home-cooked meals,
and receive information
from spirit
through orgasms, sunshine,
and broccoli sprouts.

 IF that's what you want, that's what you live ... OR you can
keep reading headlines and merely talking about change and
transformation and chasing the next shooting. (The metaphysics
of all things)

XLVI

Often pain
only lies within the repetitive thoughts.

Observe your thoughts. Then reframe them
and serve your body into greater sweetness as a result.

Sweet thoughts +sweeter thoughts =the sweetest experiences

*Take a sweet bath infused with oranges, strawberries, and mangoes.
Save sum fruit yum-ness to eat later! Submerge your whole body
and sometimes it may be necessary to submerge your whole life.
Release the day (moment, life) into your bathwater. Unplug the
drain and observe the day float away from your feet. Rinse newness
with a lukewarm to cold shower. Oh observe how the cool water
tightens your pores. Witness your heartbeat. Congrats you made it
through the rough day. You should rest well now.*

Tomorrow's newness has arrived. Get juicy over that!

XLVII—GET PREGGO WITH YOUR AND/OR LOVER'S DREAMS!

Relationships don't have to be hard or painful. Absolutely nothing 'wrong' with hard and/or painful relationships as ALL EMOTIONS and EXPERIENCES resonate with the divine and sacred. However, per usual, you always have a choice as a divine creator of ALL your experiences. No victims are allowed at this junction of your transformation! Cast a spell into your womb on behalf of the lover who enters your body. If a body can create a baby, it can also create the relationships that the owner desires and manifests dreams for everyone involved in the sexual experience.

Blooming Tip

Manifest dreams and create anything desired inside healthy pussy

Implant your dreams into me, lover
I am just that fertile.

When your womb-pussy energy is healthy, your lover can impregnate his/her dreams inside your body temple through intercourse and penetration. Or you can impregnate your dreams through self-penetration.

Before the sexual experience, get amped and deeply charged up about your dreams. Your lover should recite his/her dreams to himself/herself or for more activation energy, he or she can recite them out loud into your body. You should do the same. This encounter should take place during ovulation. It should be during a time when your breasts feel bountiful and sensitive to the touch, and your nipples ache to be sucked into the softest surrender. You should be moist in the mouth, yoni (pussy), anus, anywhere there is a hole for receptivity. You should feel radiant and alive. Consider decorating your body with beads, gold chains, crystals, or red clay like the temple that it is. All four of your lips should be swollen and your mouth should be wet, desirous of being fed your lover's creamy light. You should be ripe, glistening, soiled in your panties. Your throat should be open, exposed, and primed to sing songs, hymnals, and praises. Your eyes should be moist, ready to cry out river waters from the ecstatic worship. When your lover releases into your body (your mouth, throat, anus, pussy, the pores of your nipples, etc.), you take the energy into you, burst open with gratitude that your and your lover's and/or your dreams are coming true.

Treat your body temple with gentle care for the next 9 months, as if you are pregnant with a baby. In fact, you are pregnant with dream-babies. Take (food-based) prenatal vitamins, tell your friends to check-in on you, have a baby shower, become rounder and juicer like the moon. Wear loose fitting clothes. Tell your coworkers you are pregnant without any other details. If you are wild, quit your job, personally I didn't need it anymore. And in 9 months, give birth.

This is an ancient tool of manifestation given to me by the ancestors. It is very special to me and has transformed my life. Please enjoy the process and don't just read the words, but put the words into action.

XLVIII

What contributes to healthy vagina?

1. Water, Juices, Herbal bitter teas such as dandelion, and probiotics

2. Kind and generous touch (from yourself AND a lover or lovers)

3. Words of Praise shared with your pussy. Oh yes there is a consciousness in the vagina portal

4. Eating 'feminine' foods (more on this later and very randomly in this book)

5. MANAGING STRESS (I think this is single-handedly the most important contribution however this book is out of order and sequence, just like a woman when she is walking in her feminine power.) Being logical, rational, and in sequence is masculine and of course necessary and accessible, but constant states of masculine energy taxes the yoni/womb/vagina and yield hormonal imbalances.

6. Herbal baths and steaming your vaginal-hole (dark hole, greatest mystery), simply squatting over a pot of boiling water and inhale through your vagina's mouth or hole.(Mmm)

7. Panty-free, pant- free, and/or tampon-free living

8. Less cheese, processed milk, fried foods, SUGARY SNACKS, white bread, pre-packaged food, white potatoes, yellow pasta, and anything genetically modified. More feminine foods *giggles* See #4 for details

9. Belief that you are healthy and the courage to follow through with other healthy thoughts and beliefs

"If it can exist in your imagination, it is real. If you can't afford it, imagine it. One day you look up and your reality has reconfigured to what's been imagined. Look at you actualizing your God, your Obatala, your creative power." —India Ame'ye

BLOOMING TIP

If someone asked me for a discount, I would restate the value of my work to them, and most importantly to myself—as they are reflecting my internal conflicts. Even with my "ask for donations for my book project," I felt entitled to be donated to, and I am confident that mindset placed me in a position to receive MORE than what I asked for. Feel the entitlement in your anus portal, and let that feeling make you smile. Let go of everything else. If you worked a traditional 9-5 job, you would feel entitled to your paycheck on Friday and there would be no negotiating around that. Entrepreneurs and artists should consider adopting that same mindset! "Entitlement" has been misrepresented as arrogance—or perhaps arrogance as misrepresented as bad. But the greater point is knowing who you are and what your worth is. And being courageous enough not to negotiate around that.

 Entitlement for Artists and Those Who Are Bravely Self-employed

XLIX

...Get off that person's facebook page.
Stop reading top news stories.
Don't ruminate over the same ol' thoughts.
Let go of the past. Most importantly tell your body it's ok to let go.
...Stop calling her then.
You don't have to bring your co-worker home in your head.
If you eat it, love it. If you don't love it, don't eat it. This applies to
every area of your life beyond food.
Don't look for reasons to get more pissed off.
Invoke more reasons to embody love,
share love, experience love, eat love, and pledge your allegiance to
love. What you focus on grows like wild flowers in the earth's soil
(soul). I dare you to water your body, become more juicy, and grow
more love.

 **Water Your Body, Become More
Juicy, and Grow More Love**

L

I just want to love you

and keep it just that simple.

Love is easy. Possession disguised as love is complicated and increases internal and external suffering.

a

My breasts are ripe
with many stars.
non possessive
kind of love.

-Abundance vs Scarcity

The whole idea is to start telling new stories. Sink into your imagination. Sip on the enchantment. Straddle the bliss. Start now.

LI

Divine timing is the
only real time
for bending spoons to stir in magic and miracles, to sit in warm stillness knowing
all is well and right on time, simply
…when it's time, it- is-on- time.
No worries or stress in the cells, just
loving thoughts inside organs
as prayers. Allowing the energy to
build on a path that it's already going.
When it arrives, drop down into your joy and remember:
'This fragrant flower is the memory
of the heirloom seeds I've been sowing.'

————

I'm not concerned about letting my roommate have some coconut oil for her needs. Use my extra virgin organic coconut ($44.99 per jar) up because I'm so confident in my supply from Whole foods Market, literally walking distance from my backyard. I am confident that I can go anytime I desire with the appropriate resources in hand and buy some more. And more . . . and MORE . And we CAN both glow and be radiant from USING the abundant supply coconut oil, as my roommate's radiance is my radiance; we are both breathing the same air. She responded "I wish I could afford this stuff?!" and I'm seeing myself in her, channeling a similar place within me, to remind myself that we are indeed breathing the same air AND there's always a jar of this stuff in the house. Owning the reality (without saying a word to her) that she CAN indeed afford it because it's always HERE, in the cabinet, ready for her to use. And there' s always more from where that came from.

Coconut Abundance Story

107

LII

How I healed my fibroids and the accompanying painful, heavy moon cycles?

I thought it was normal to bleed heavy. My mum and sister did. My friends did. Their mothers did. We always had boxes of overnight pads hidden in the linen closet and expected to wear them uncomfortably during the day. I couldn't remember ever having a period where I didn't need the pad turned diaper around my second day of bleeding. Moreover the dread of bleeding for 8-10 days, maybe even bleeding between moons was a drag. I spent many cycles moody, aggravated, and riddled in cramps. While in undergrad I spent hours being sedated with pain killers in my university's infirmary, awaken by my then boyfriend to be driven back to my dorm room. Even he was accustomed to this monthly "period" routine. I remember one time we were taking a road trip, and he had to find a place for me to change my pad every 45 minutes or so. I was bleeding golf-ball size clots at 19 years old.

One day while giving me a massage, this same boyfriend found a lump in my lower belly area. It was a small one but I was still embarrassed about it. He had discovered my fibroid, possibly fibroids, and the reason why intercourse with him had become painful. I remember my sister telling me that 15 years ago she had some fibroids and cysts removed from her body. The women in my family gathered and charged up around common issues with their bodies so having challenging in my lady parts felt pretty normal (at that time). *Not now though because I not only rewrote my story, I rewrote their stories as well.*

I started rewriting my stories around 21. I guess some people would say that I was telling lies. Giggles! Here's the 3-D punch! Every "rewrite" I told has come into fruition now because deep down I always knew that there was MORE to my being, who I am beyond what was experienced or communicated by family and friends. Other dimensions at play. Therefore I am no longer the same person I was genetically, emotionally, physically, physiologically, spirituality, or hormonally nearly 20 years ago.

I also started to work out in a gym, shape and contour my structure. Stumbling into Gold's Gym for the 1st time was intriguing and scary. But it helped me to witness how focused concentration on bodily goals was a shapeshifting ritual. Incorporating shapeshifting ritual meant that I can redesign my body to be, do, or experience whatever it was I desired. I desired to live in a body temple that was fibroid free with an impeccable digestive and immune systems and soft but firm muscle mass. As a result my body removes waste a few times per day which I believe creates an internal harmony that doesn't allow excess waste and mucous to accumulate and therefore fibroids to grow. I don't have empirical proof nor am I doctor, but I am clear that the aforementioned helped heal my most sacred and tastiest mystery. You know what else? It's also having command over your body, even the confidence to state your desires for the body you desire to live in, knowing that you are SO worthy of those things and will do what it takes to attract those desires.

And the last thing that helped to heal my fibroids was shifting my pallet to eating quality food. Notice I didn't say vegan or vegetarian, and while I eat a large amount of organic veggies, I am very clear that a plant-based diet is not the harmony for this body temple. I eat like a country girl too—For an example this morning I had a green smoothie, organic yellow grits cooked in local lard, raw milk, himalayan salt, and organic butter with salmon croquettes also cooked in lard and coconut oil and sliced mango. It was so delish! So while I have an awareness of my dairy intake, I only eat quality dairy without hormones or antibodies, the closest food our great grandmamas used to eat. Also I walk/jog/bike, dance, stretch and contour my limbs in otherworldly positions, and squat to root my energy. I like to keep my energy flowing because stagnate energy is a breeding ground to harvest fibroids instead of blooms.

No doctors or no surgeries for me either. A shift in how I was processing life, reaching for the most loving and healing thoughts, and trusting ALL my emotions, even those emotions or experiences that don't feel so loving and letting them know that every bit of me is still valid and worship-able. The most stressed I had in the last two years has been working in a natural foods grocery store as an assistant manager. I no longer work there and I am managing my prosperity through seeding my trust daily that I can earn a living off my divine gifts.

Also I don't *fuck in fear*, which means that I only share intimacy in the presence of the holy spirit of love. That doesn't mean that my lover and I will be together forever, but it does mean that a heart-connection has been established first which allows my sacred medicine to flow into my lover, and creates an open pathway for my lover's medicine to enter into me. Sex is merely an exchange of medicine, the healing lies in the energetic bodies and in my 30s, I learned to only allow love inside through deep throat purrs, moans, thrusts, sweat, tears, and breasts and ass bounces --on the inhale-- with my lover. No condoms, dentals dams, or any other "protection" allowed; I am always safe...but I have worked really deeply to be this way.

Ultimately it was through a radical life style change I healed my fibroids. I started juicing twice a day—and not because I was trying to heal myself but my tastebuds shifted, so I was far more thirsty for fresh juice, lemon water, and herbal teas than food. I have zero cramps or any other painful tendencies. Also I eat really streamlined versions of dairy, choosing raw, local milk, local eggs, and raw, local butter over the alternatives. And I move my ass daily. Some days, hourly.

LIII

We are all "using" one another—sweet manipulators, Oshun incarnates, energy archetypes, magical beings, forest nymphs, honey in tow, finely dressed beings appealing to senses of humanity.

We use plants for nutrients and the earth uses humanity to distribute oxygen.

You have so much love to give —that you are being "used" for that love, brilliantly used for love. You are giving AND receiving love and when you can do this holy act without care, concern, or worry about the outcome, you will see you lover return your calls. All your desires are met inside this sweetest surrender.

Eventually I learned that.

Let go. Redirect your focuses. And get your sheer dress ready for the celebration.

~For women who feel like they have been or are being "used" and ignored~

At some point you have to get rid of everything that keeps you from seeing yourself as a loving being, a sexual being, an abundant being, and a spiritual experience and prance around with your breasts out accordingly.

LIV

Sometimes

most of the "work" is

learning to stand still,

silently and alone,

without clothes,

under moonlight,

and simply be astonished

by what you feel.

Dig deeper into feeling

Blooming Tip

One of the reasons I go off into the woods is not to collect my thoughts, but to surrender my thoughts and consequently liberate my life force. Take the beauty into my body, listen to the symphony of sounds, marvel in the shared abundance, witness the animals movements, dance with the trees and wind, and taste the salt of the earth on my skin. *And when I return to my own thinking, I am changed.*

LV

I feel like when I'm giving head,

I'm doing God's work.

How do you feel when you are giving head?
Write it out or draw a picture

_____

_____

_____

_____

LVI

..Because I believe more in love. I receive love into my body and reality. Frankly love-making—in ALL its expressions-is my brand of activism and contribution to the planet. I don't watch/listen/hear many programmings of the media, but I do listen to the seat of my soul, the melody of my orgasm, and effortlessly dance with trees. Think of children: free people! They hold more intense passion for what they love than what they don't. If children were activists then their activism (i.e. purpose and passions) would mirror whatever they love, instead of what they don't.

I think you have to make the conscious choice to see something else, something different from what you were taught, and that sight creates your reality and influences the reality of anyone that encounters you. How powerful and transformative is it that we are all connected.

~Blooming tip~

You are brave and living medicine. Strut accordingly.

~Blooming tip~

Don't wait until you are sick to start nourishing and taking care of yourself.

LVII

Lately when I take self-portraits, I can't tell if it's 2014 or 1812. That's the beauty of photography and somehow the DNA that runs in my bones and blood reveals itself in the most opportune times.

My Aunt Gemma, "Gem" for short, a highly charged, wealthy, liberated African woman, taught me what a round ass, curvy body, and raw in-step do for humanity. She had such a BIG personality and attraction about her, even in her shyness. I learned to shape and cultivate my curves like ritual through watching her dance and play with her body. Oftentimes when I am alone in bed, she crawls into my dreams, like we are both on tele-vision, perhaps 'telling-me-vision,' just to help me remember. She constantly affirms how worthy I am of deep intimacy and pleasure. She reminds me to be wild, free, and untamed, that my spirits needs to be fully self-expressed in order to access my powers and mysteries. She taught me how my breasts are power lines to the divine ... 'don't pray like most people ... pray to your titties.' She puts me at ease when I get possessed by the holy spirit of love. She was born in 1812 and lives left- of-center through me.

Wait! She is me.

~Aunt Gemma: A Deeper Truth~

Blooming Tip

Why is it that many of the movements that felt natural to twirl in as a child, we stop doing those same moves as an adult? Also remember how we would pull our dresses over our heads, take off all our clothes, twist our hips and bottoms, and be sassy. We were called so many names we stopped doing those things.

So here's what I do. When I go for a walk in the city streets, I feel my hips and ass, and I command attention. I walk "womanly." I twist. I smile. I ride my own sass. Command my safety to do so. See everyone as my protectors and making space for my healing. Or if I don't feel like smiling, I do whatever it is I need to do so that my body knows that I'm its owner and available to meets its needs. Sometimes I walk and pretend the sun is shining out of my booty. Sounds silly, eh, but that ability to see your body as otherworldly mythology, without fears or shame around that, and tap into your ability to harness the shapes that your body desires to live in, like play-do, because you hold command over your body temple. Oh lets not forget about the full body orgasms. Juicy genitals. Blood circulating light. Healed organs. Are you still laughing, Beloved?

Also I decorated my hips and ass, with flower while laying naked on the bed or sprinkles of glitter, body chains and cowrie shells. I like to make sound when I walk from one room into another.

Welp now my ass is the size of two full moons. Energy surely does go where attention flows. Abundance resting within and translating in every area of my life.

~Sip this green juice below with your head tilted back~

Ancestors speak the language of intuition and symbols through the elements, memories, dreams, and metaphors. If you want them to be active in your life, all it takes is generous intention and outward celebration in their royal honor. They are always around, desiring to be in service to you by way of being honorably possessed by you. To go into possession means to be utilized as a channel by those benevolent ancestors so that information can have movement and flow freely into your body temple and out into the Earth. This spirited dance reduces the possibility of information dying and decaying with the deceased. Instead information is given voice and fuel and air to expand into greater consciousness. I channel through sound (singing), lovemaking, nature play, and writing. What ways do you channel? It's OK not to know how you channel, consider starting with the actions and activities that take you out-of your mind and into deeper layers of your body temple. Also how do you celebrate your multicultural ancestors? Sometimes you may feel intense ties to people you don't really know in the physical world or people you may not have a name for. Josephine Baker is one of my ancestors but I can't tell you how/why. Also my Aunt Gemma, who taught me what a round ass and curvy body do for the consciousness of humanity, is my dear ancestor. I have never met Aunt Gemma and no one else "knows" Aunt Gemma, but she came to me years ago in a few dreams and sits bravely on my altar without any concerns or questions. I also have various cultures of African ancestors, Indian ancestors, Japanese ancestors, and Latin, Mexican, Peruvian, Brazilian, and European Ancestors, as my love and adoration for certain art, fabrics, music, films, music, and foods trigger their memories. Eventually you come to place where any person who dies has the capacity to be a potential ancestor which begets the question "Are we all here as returning ancestors simply honoring and celebrating ourselves?"

LVIII

My experiences have been that it takes time and patience. Allow yourself to FEEL the range of emotions that show up without judgment, guilt, or shame. When you are ready, find a radical self-care *practice* that you can consistently implement into your healing process. Also when you are ready, delight in a space of gratitude for your "ex-lover." Indeed she or he helped you to evolve and showed you pieces of yourself, parts of you that may have been difficult for you to own and participated in your growth. Also your "ex" is and probably will always be a part of your life; just one thought activates memory in the body, so instead of forever aching within, allow yourself to feel joy and beauty for those experiences—this will take time, beloved ... but it can happen. This feeling of joy will permeate in every cell of your body. Get active, definitely move your hips, breasts, belly, ass, and get excited about the possibility of "new" love, which is actually simply "more" self-love. Relationships are continuums in life's journeys, so consider adding love and value where ever you go, and witness your impending magnetism in your life. The more magnetic you are, the more you raise your energetic frequency to attract and manifest anything you desire. Be gentle with yourself, Anonymous. Just asking this question is a powerful start.

Question from Anonymous blog reader "How to get over a breakup?"

All transformation and fun come
after the breakup:
the opportunity to allow
those qualities you want
to manifest
in a lover or lovers (if you so choose)
to show up
within your blood
and bones. Those who you love
are simply mirrors. How clean is yours?

Clean mirrors: Breakups are acts of radical self-love/care

LVIX

Being a Goddess, which extends far outside of the gender binary, means that you are so confident, trusting, and connected that you don't need to worry about a thing. You surrender with ease knowing when to maneuver out of the way and allow the angels to do their work. You're free to simply to be beautiful, magical, and inside uninhibited pleasure.

~Be a Goddess Beloved. But only you can determine what that Goddess looks like for you...as you~

I create drenched in wetness. So flushed with pleasurable heat that I birth songs, unearth beats, write lyrics, and take breaks to make food to feed my creative deity of fire and desire while listening to the lyrics of sappy love songs and songs contains flutes, horns, and drums to nourish me into my writing adventures. I am so far from being lonely. I am unquestionably sustained by love as the holy spirit of love. I am convinced that experiencing love stories is medicinal and writing about love stories and the accompanied love-making are tools of transformation. I try to express that when I write, I experience a 4-directional hormonal surge; it's all serotonin, oxytocin, DHEA, and other unmentionable pleasure hormones from there. I am thinking how awesome we get to experience love and experience that moment again in retrospect through writing, music, movies, people, and celebratory memories.....Uh-oh, the veil's lifting; the portals are opening again. Going back into possession...it's the takeover, sun. Petals of rain I leave in the kitchen.

LX

After all this time of
desiring a healing lover,
I now understand how learning to
unearth the Goddess from my root chakra
taught me deeply about love and pleasure.
Not in an effort to be isolated or celibate,
but to affirm in my blood, bones, and cellular memory
how worthy I am of intense, rapturous pleasure
and true (unconditional) love.
My lover has been here the entire time
seeking nothing but its enchanted curvy self.
With this awareness, I am now
ready and capable of sharing
with unfathomable beauty and exemplary grace,
my abundant love,
charming sweetness,
unique sacred gifts,
and juicy magnetism
inside the magic of another.

Veins of Raw Honey

LXI

There can be a grand and royal difference between a mistress and "a-woman-fucking-some-woman's-husband (or partner) on the side." A mistress blooms inside mystery. She listens and heals with her beating heart, which is part of the reason she is so attractive. She moves in her feminine graces and all men, most men, many women, most people, are attracted to her high-priestess ease...in some way. A mistress teaches us to harness the courage to be present with any moment; she has nothing to gain or lose. Whether she physically acts on the attraction or not ... is irrelevant because hubby will continue to think of her, and subsequently ignite a connection, an energetic connection which is just as powerful, if not more powerful than a physical one. No one can stop her wild feminine fire, glowing in her divinity, so any wife would be in service to herself to work on her own magnetism and get her fire up, not in competition, but in an effort to integrate all the life force that is needed for herself and her community. So whether you are a wife, mistress, or whatever, please know you are valuable and ... sacred. When you are ready, you can let go the guilt, shame, blame, sadness, victimhood, etc., and see the beauty that lies in ALL experiences. The mistress is a part of your community; she has always been a part of your community. She provides a service ... a comfort worthy of learning from, desired nourishment from her divine mystery. See her as that mistress. You can do this ... if you choose.

Her Story, Your story, One Experience

Reframing experiences into higher vibrations of love (How to heal the hurt by bringing new lenses to an old story permanently photographed in your subconscious mind)

An FYI: I have never been sexual connected with anyone's husband. I have been cheating on, and I wish I had tools in reframing stories when I was glowing through the mire

LXII

"HOW ADORABLE THAT ALL THIS TIME SACRED SEXUALITY HAS BEEN ONE OF THE
GREATEST WAY TO SIMPLY COMMUNICATE WITH THE DIVINE?"-INDIA AME'YE

I have always possessed a high sexual energy...always sensual and kinesthetic even
as a child. But it was frowned upon, censored, and reduced to heavy periods and
the inability to 'feel' deeply in my early teens. I became terribly repressed, dying
in the belief that I was "wrong" or "different" or "not enough." I spent many
years ashamed and confused about who I was..feeling thoroughly unaccepted
and misinformed. And then I learned (and continue to learn) to accept myself
fully and completely for who I am *to the best of my abilities*, waning and waxing
in a space of non-judgment. I think it started with my self-portraits, learning to
adore my bits and pieces. I now embrace my sexuality, whatever that is and bask

in the radiance, power, and deliciousness of my body temple. No longer am I a prisoner of my strict Nigerian-Southern Black American upbringings. I am free! As a past lover once said to me, "You are the freest person I know." I took her words into my organs as medicine and beautifully saved myself from cancer. My body temple is so open now that it moves into arousal over the wonder of a single sunrise.

LXIII

Condition yourself

to feel pleasure

inside your trauma.

Recall the traumatic memory.

Invite pleasure to come alongside

the feeling of trauma until pleasure becomes

more accessible than the trauma.

Energy manipulation is changing the impact of one thing and replacing it with something else

Darlin' celebrate your fertility. If you don't have fertility, crops can't grow.

LXIV

SENSUALITY

SIMPLY THE CAPACITY TO FEEL

Lets honor your feelings. What do you feel in your body right now? _____

_____

LXV

When a woman is in her most transformative state, her eyes radically change. She not only awakens her 3rd eye but also accesses deeper dimensions in her yoni portal. Don't be surprised if she speaks rapidly—("speaking in tongues'"as they say in baptist churches) or if her mouth gets wetter and more pronounced. This sacred sight is prime evidence that she has allowed herself to be possessed by the holy spirit of love or Oshun or_____ (insert whatever deity or animal spirit she carries within her heart). Nothing to do at that point, but draw, write, sing, cry, bathe, or fuck. Anything she touches in this heightened state receives a charge and sacred information. Activated women don't need herb or alcohol to access this portal. It's a different kind of "flight" when a woman taps into and leads with her abundant heart. Don't be alarmed, lovers. If she touches you, she magnetizes you. A magnetic lover is a success ... always and in all ways. It's really a celebration of transformation and your impending prosperity to even be near her.

 When a person makes love to Goddess, that person is in her/his prosperity. Therefore when your lover makes love to you, your lover becomes far more abundant than when he or she first encountered you.

Take that attitude and energy into your pussy and breath chile.

Don't be bashful. To be empowered to speak and heal your throat (voice), consider learning how to truly eat pussy and/or suck dick and allow yourself to uninhibitedly receive when being served in this way. You will find your unique psalms, the voice of the divine, during the exercise of tasting and restorative rest of letting go. The reality that no two people could ever occupy the same voice is power + alchemy to be utilized for transformation.

--Throat Chakra Exercises

There was a total focus upon my being, not my mind or thoughts, or the bed or counter we laid on. It was a presence of being that had nothing to do with time or space. Sometimes in lovemaking I would be completely succumb and have to stop and take a deep breath because I couldn't feel where my body stopped or hers began. There would be this oneness. Fire at the core of flames. A blaze of heat, softness, and wet magic. Licking wildly, rhythmic kissing, the art of two bellies and 4 breasts cummin' and glowin' at the same time. Fleshy hips rotating, egos undernourished.

LXVI

7 steps to becoming more orgasmic

Take creative action to become more vulnerable and profoundly open like a child or perhaps a tree, you choose! It can be through dance, photography, journaling, or crocheting in full blown sunshine with your legs wide open.

Visualize yourself as a child being encouraged to express. Consider creating an altar to your inner child and speaking (with power ... that's so important) about your body parts and how you feel. This could seem silly (*oh but it's ok to be silly, right?*) ... See your parents or any other adult affirming you, like 'good job <u>insert your name</u>, I am so proud of you for expressing _____,' This is a very simple way of reprogramming your cells, tissues, and organs. bit by bit. vision by vision. 3rd-eye brilliancy!

Be encouraged to talk more openly about your pussy. Understand your pussy is just as worthy of being heard from as your right arm.

Check in with your receptive pussy ... It was created to receive! What does your pussy need to receive? Radical self-care? Your kind touch? To experience a healthy dick, another healthy pussy, or a combination of both? Or to feel sunshine, the trees, stars, or any other natural wonder? A yogurt flush? Some natural soap? Or cucumber medicine? More water or dandelion tea in your body temple? Words of Affirmation? To be worshipped and supported by a healing lover? Whatever it is...check in and shift accordingly.

Engage more action steps: Touch yourself until you laugh or cry or feel love, or anger, or sadness or some other emotion other than numbness. Don't judge whatever emotion comes up for you. If you feel something that in and of itself is a call and response for celebration.

Practice moaning. *Wait don't just practice—ritualize it.* Hold your head back, open your throat, allow your consciousness to drop down into your throat, and moan from the depths of your inner child. Affirm your right to experience pleasure from this place. Feel the connection from your throat to your pussy to your anus. A great exercise to do at your inner child altar. You are bursting your root chakra open to receive pleasure.

When you bathe or shower, *notice how sensitive you are to the soap, the sponge, the water temperature and pressure ... don't do anything, but merely notice.* You are strengthening your awareness of your body temple. You are signing your permission slip to explode into a tsunami.

Goddess don't overlook the orgasms happening within your throat.

LXVII

I don't know what it is but most days I twirl around in full blown arousal or damn near arousal, delightfully easily aroused. That arousal is rarely connected to sex or intimacy with another person, but to the most mundane of things I experienced while alone. It goes like this: cleaning the veggies turns into watching how the water streams out of the faucet and covers the veggies. Feeling the wetness on the leaves as I flip the veggies over and under giggling from being splashed in the face. Hearing the roar of the juicer coming on, then using the plunge to thrust the veggies through the juicer, witnessing the veggies transform from matter into liquid. Observing this life force release into my cup, sometimes even overflowing with abundance. And making myself sit down, in the quiet, doing absolutely nothing else— and tasting every bit without any distractions. Most days it takes 10 minutes to drink one glass of juice. but I am not merely "drinking," I am becoming ... the juice ... nutritious and delicious. Bursting magic. Possessed by the juice I drink.

~Juice Possession~

LXVIII

A woman's body was not birthed to move in straight lines. When you walk, hold that energy.

Her breasts are ripe

with many stars,

a non possessive

kind of love.

~Full of stars

LXIX

People are unconsciously drawn to magnetic people. Frankly, they can't help themselves. Consider it an offering when people find themselves attracted to you, as attraction is only a product of energy. When a person desires to extend her/himself to you, it is a gifted reflection! Even if the person is seemingly annoying, misses the mark, doesn't have as much money as you require, or just isn't attractive to you, s/he can be stripped down to her or his heart, in other words, deconstructed to the core of love and embraced in that safe space. That is a woman's power to create safe spaces in others, in any place she chooses.

With that understanding, we can draw a lover or lovers to us just by letting the most abundant universe know we are deeply open to receive. Sometimes when energies feel uncomfortable or uneasy, the draw or pull comes from our higher self, a place that is all-knowing and connected to supreme consciousness, or what I refer to as, Goddess consciousness. Our higher selves always know more than other parts of our be-ing. Our spirits see beyond what's in sight and attract to us experiences or human spirits that (can) grow us, love us ... help heal us deeply. And guess what, our higher self doesn't consider relationship status. The higher self could care less if you are married or single! That is an affirmation for having the divine choice to be open to present moment, what lies before you, without trekking far off into the past or future, and being open to receive subsequent transformations ... into our greater selves ... when we are simply humble enough to receive and allow.

Rather than having a goal of orgasm, consider surrendering into optimal sensation, and before you know it, you will have exploded into starry night, holy night.

LXX

Set your desires free...

even if only in a love poem.

———

LXXI

2 Trees Meditation

Lover 1 imagines breathing up from the earth through her/his anus portal, breathing that energy up from the base of her/his spine and exhaling the energy out of her/his mouth and into the mouth of Lover 2. Lover 2 receives the shotgun of energy into her/his mouth, opens her/his throat while tilting her/his head back and exhaling the energy down her/his throat and into the spine, out of her/his anus, and into the warm transformative of the earth. Imagine the experience as a bowel movement, a great release. They continue in this manner until Lover #1 feels present, available, hard/wet, relaxed, and cleared in her/his body then switch positions.

LXXII

*When a Goddess dares to ejaculate,
to engage her amrita fluids and accompanying spells,
she taps into the magic and ministry
of her very own body temple.*

—Church of the Living Goddess by (India Ame'ye)

Simple Steps to Ejaculation (There are many more!)

1. Surrender into the present moment. During intimacy and love-making, nothing else matters.

2. Drop down into whatever you feel and receive pleasure. Affirm your right to receive pleasure.

3. Engage undulations and push your clitoris and the accompanying orgasm outward.

4. Try not to be so contained and pretty. Actually leave your ego; growl, purr, slob, cry, just allow your body to do what it needs to do to get you there. Trust your body and give it permission to spray its holy water onto your lover, the sheets or walls, or anything else within sight.

LXXIII

Oftentimes
when I am cleaning floors,
yes,
cleaning ... floors...,
I am doing so
with full joy
and sensual delight.
Grateful to be in
a healthy red clay body
with knees that bend
without fail
and
a spine that curls
when commanded.
Nude or
barely covered.
Juicy and ignited.
Cleaning
floors with my bare brown hands
and freshly-washed white towels.

No mop, please.

Only Thelonious Monk
blasting from speakers
and homemade
lemon soap heightening
my senses.
I am mopping
floors with my bare hands.
Receiving information.
Interpreting reality.
Feeling my way into orgasm.
Creating my own pleasures!
Remembering and RECONSTRUCTING.
Needlessly to say, I love clean floors.

Orgasmic living in practice

LXXIV

SENSUAL YONI (VAGINA) TEA:

Calendula, Lemon, Rose, marshmallow root,
wormwood, rosemary (1 tsp each) to a large pot (½ gallon of water)

Bring to a boil. Place pot on floor on top of a towel or sheet. Squat over pot.
Careful not to touch the rim.

Breathe steam into your organs through your yoni or vaginal mouth. Drink the
tea up your spine. Become the steam. Feel into the experience. I steam my yoni
portal 1-2 days after the last day of moon cycle.

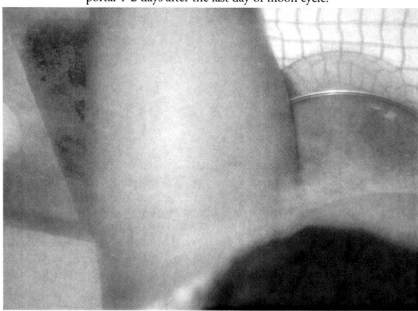

*Darlin' be sorcerer of love, where everything you touch turns into love. NOT
"love" as a concept in your mind but love as a total body tantric experience.*

LXXXV

Can I say that my sex drive has been higher than all my lovers, partly because I've always done other simple activities that bring me pleasure, even before I understood what was taking place. In my early 30s, most of these things took place in nature e.g. sunbathing, nude hiking, nude dancing in desolate forests, visualizations, body cultivation, and breathing rituals/celebrations, shaking and releasing exercises, along with butt and thigh 'exercises' that should be more appropriately termed 'sacral and root chakra openers,' sweetness baths, even organizing and cleaning (picking up trash in nature as my offering to MAMA). So the pleasure extracted from everyday life feels very similar to having sex. Basically I'm fucking all the time, and while I adore passionate sex and deep ecstasy, discovering orgasmic pleasure easily and everywhere, at any time, means that my body is alive and receptive yet doesn't necessarily rely on a sexual partner to cum, heal, and transform.

--Beloved: Please cum, heal, transform

LXXVI

There is a metaphysical component to all perceived sexual diseases and illnesses in general. Essentially what you believe becomes what you receive. The root cause of STDs lies deeply inside of fear-based beliefs and the accompanying fear-based actions. If you have sex with someone, you have to embody love, overflow with love, and LOVE him/her. Otherwise you unconsciously embody fear, which creates a chemistry between you two that attracts illness and disease. Condoms, dental dams, spermicides, birth control pills and other related plastics and chemicals are essential for people who have sex in the presence of fear. Loving someone, not to be confused with possessing someone, only brings more love into the body.

Fear and love are the only two vibrations you can encounter in any experience, sexual experience included. If sex doesn't include love and loving, be sure to wear a dental dam and/or condom. If you have not established a heart connection with your intimate partner and feel some type of fear around that, be sure to wear a dental dam and/or condom.

LXXVII

The feminine force is a creative, wild, enchanting energy that feeds all life. To be in any way opposed to it is to annihilate our fundamental being at the cellular level. It's a quality and essence that not only resides in women, but in men and all humans beautifully between and beyond the constructions of gender.

Mama Earth embodies divine sacred feminine as the earth nourishes every cell of our being and support the unseen colorful dimensions of ourselves.

It's in renewing our very natural connection to the earth that we learn how to develop the more evolved versions of ourselves.

--Feminine force of nature

LXVIII

Blooming tip

Create your own love manifesto

I am an independent contractor of love. I am so fierce with my divinity that my love for you is not based on your love for me. I don't need your reciprocity or support. Your holds and barriers on love don't mean a thing to me; I am going to love you ... because ... well, I LOVE you. And in loving you, I am loving me, as what I see in you is a reflected version of me, like how the moon reflects sunlight.

 unconditionallovemanifesto:

The result of living inside an activated body and embodying love is that you are capable of truly loving. You will have many moments, days, weeks, and lifetimes where you will be able to love unconditionally, and not just with your children either.

LXXIX

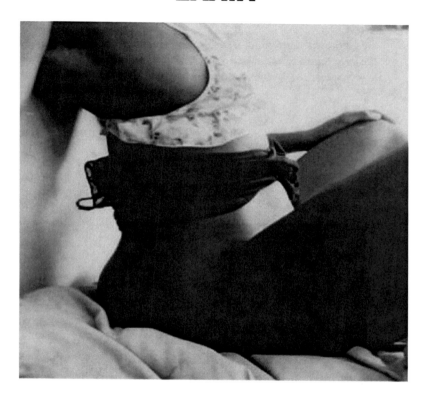

My sensuality has nothing
to do with men.
my expression of my sensuality
has nothing to do with men.
my sensuality
(and all the ways it expresses itself)
has everything to do with me.
everything I am
and every way that I am
is deliberate
and intentional as I live to
shapeshift my curves and cultivate my body in ritual.

-de(liberate)

LXXX

Be loud with your unique songs, words, laughter, and declarations. Allow your life to make noise and take up space. When you turn a corner, deliver wideness in your stance. Make sure your hips know that they are worthy of being noticed so that they won't cower, shrink, and go away.

.loud, wide, and greatly noticed

LXXXI

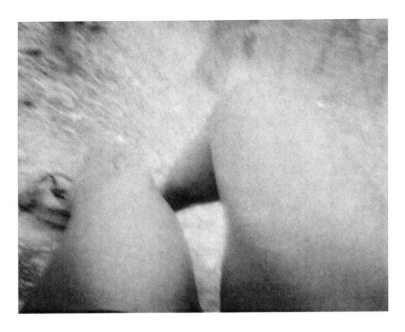

It is essential to go whole days without thinking too much about a thing.

LXXXII

Sing into the pores of your skin:

My body is intelligent and trust-worthy.

**I remind myself that the moon swings
inside me every month.
And act accordingly.**

Blooming Tip

When was the last time you had sex?

Five minutes ago. I made all sorts of love with my wild salmon and pineapple-curry-coconut sauce drizzled over an enormous amount of steamed local veggies and aromatic turmeric jasmine rice eaten out my favorite bamboo bowl and a 16 oz. fresh organic cucumber and ginger juice. I had sex outside too…on the patio in this really comfy chair. Every cell of my body was deliciously penetrated in warm, spicy de-light. Thanks for your question, Anon! I love sex at all times so much so that I seemingly can never stop having it. You should have heard me with my watermelon juice this morning. *I live in a sustained orgasm.*

LXXXIII

I feel most feminine
when I'm sucking on his healing wand slowly.
On my knees. Ass stuck out into galaxies.
Messy 3D hair. Sticky face and hands.
Wetness from my protruding mouth.
Hungry from rabid wild desire.
Performing Goddess duties
in prayer position to H.I.M.
With a lake of tears forming in my eyes
And a gushing river running down my thighs.
In service to his healing
and simultaneously my own.
We burst into stars. Together."

 One of the gazillion benefits of giving amazing head is encountering the moment when you realize that it CAN be more than just 'giving head,' it is 'giving heart.' The profundity in giving is that giving is indeed a sacred act of receiving, profound activation of the heart. One person's healing is another person's healing and how perfect that healing would happen in the heart chakra, which is why sex rooted in a heart connection heals.

LXXXIV

"Darlin' are you not cummin' and calling yourself alive too?" -India Ame'ye

Women are the most powerful natural resources on the planet.
Women are wild transformative forces of nature.
But how many of us have become tidy, neat, quiet, acceptable versions of ourselves when raging rivers run down our legs and below sea levels (below surfaces). We need those rivers to let loose in creative expression and bodacious action.

How can you be of service?

Women

145

LXXXV

She ADORES the sensual nature of being outdoors daily (opportunities to feel, touch, smell, and be at one with nature, the essence of being one with her WHOLE self).

Observing herself as a part of the natural world.

She loves the quiet, romantic feeling, hugging-kissing on trees, the wide-open spaces, the COLORS, desolate, secluded gems, the SOUNDS of twigs snapping and leaves crunching, bathing in clear lakes, bare feet on rocks, hanging on the sides of cliffs.

 Nature is a type of KAMA SUTRA in its own brilliant way! Being in nature is her deepest radical self care.

Blooming Tip

The best way to learn more about Nature is to simply play in Nature.

Get out-of-doors, outside, play in the red clay dirt, climb a tree, explore swimming holes, dance in the rain, roll in the grass, run through wild fields, wear wild flowers, delve into secret woods, admire the different smells, walk barefoot, touch trees, sing songs to the plants and vegetation, and learn about their energies and souls. Shapeshift into a bird: flap your arms and soar to your next destination without fear, worry, or concern.

LXXXVI

"How many times have you imagined something and it came to life? Imagination is alchemy. It is tuning into a different frequency, a version of yourself in another dimension and bringing the experience into the now. Allow yourself to experience the version of yourself that you'd like to be right now. The more you experience this version of yourself, the more vivid the imagined memory of self becomes who you are. Remember everything you desire has been experienced...you're just tapping into the frequency that it is happening on. Basically the memory has happened, you are merely catching up to the experience." --India Ame'ye

Folks are surprised when I tell them that at the root of all things is sex! This is a major reason I don't relate to the myth called celibacy. I know when a person is truly **alive**—feeling, sensing, questioning, creating, smiling, even observing skin tones or looking at colors —he/she are on the other side of celibacy, even if said person isn't currently having sex with another person.

When I experience nature, I realize how celibacy doesn't exist. Everything in nature extends itself into something else. Sitting or standing on the earth is a sexual experience. The root chakra is penetrated by the earth and creates the most luminous connection inside the body temple. When this happens, the body becomes a conduit for transformation and change.

Being open to nature as a lover has been a deeply transformative healing experience, so much so that I cried today. I cried in front of a child and told him I had allergies :). I wasn't brave enough in that moment to tell him the truth, and use that opportunity to reframe the power of tears in his mind. Yes I am reminded that being courageous enough to allow tears is sex too, the emotional penetration enables the soul to simply *feel* and wets up the face in the interim.

Being alive is quite sexual and serves you well.

———

LXXXVI

I will meet you at that place in your heart where you are capable of loving without conditions.

Authentic Love

GOD IS WOMB. WELCUM TO YOUR DARKNESS, THE SPACE THAT BIRTHS, REBIRTHS, AND NOURISHES ALL. QUEENLY ONE, YOU CAN HAVE WHATEVER IT IS YOU DESIRE THROUGH THE PORTAL THAT SITS BETWEEN YOUR THIGHS. MMM, THE PORTAL OF PROSPERITY AND CREATION. FEED YOUR DESIRES INTO YOUR W/HOLE...BEING. LAY BACK AND PLACE SUNFLOWERS OR WILDFLOWERS OR PINK ROSES OR CHRYSANTHEMUMS IN ITS ROYAL HONOR. SIT INSIDE GENEROUS PLANT LIFE.

LXXXVIII

I am deliriously enjoying my time with me. I don't feel single in the way did that I did in my 20s. I feel connected in many other ways, and not only to every person I ever made love to, but also to the deepest vibrations of my heart, my desires, to the earth, to how energy moves, all types of people, music, and even connected to the characters in the books I haven't finished. Even when I meet someone new and beautiful, I realize that my spirit commanded me to the stillness of this quiet space, and challenged my courage to simply sit here. Stretch. Spiral. Elongate. To do absolutely nothing. This part of my journey was necessary so much so that I attracted a "job" with the benefits of lots of quiet, introspective time, a full year to clear, heal, regenerate, and care for myself, undisturbed by fluorescent lights, noisiness, and traffic. I ... can't ... remember ... the ... last time ... I sat in traffic. I sometimes read all day long without a phone call. My higher self knows what it needs in order to shine. Sometimes I go the gym or buy a green juice without having to say much, only smile when I am ready. Or spend hours twirling my ass off in nature. I suppose I am quasi-single, but I do make love. All day. Sometimes even in my sleep. Some days I would argue that I am in the midst of a love story. Deliriously in love. This is my life ... and I always have a choice in my experiences.

So thankful that Mum walked around our house with her big ol' breasts hanging out, adoring herself as she moved. It is in my DNA to act this way.

Or was it in my DNA? Did I rewrite mum's story too and it became part of my DNA? Who knows, who cares....the fact is that I am walking around with my pointed breasts hanging out too.

LXXXIX

My mum used to embarrass me often as a young girl.

It wasn't intentional; it was her natural way of being.

Rarely did I come home from school and she was fully dressed. I prepped EVERYONE of my childhood friends before they came over, "She is not from this country ... she doesn't act like a 'normal' mum." Eventually I stopped my friends from coming over because she would lazily drape her body in an effort to relax me, but before you knew it, she'd walk into my room, talk to us about God, not realizing that the fabric was falling down and her bold titties and puffy nipples were nearly hanging out. I don't think my friends noticed it as much as I did. Mortified, I would go, 'MAAAAH' and she'd turn around and rewrap herself, this time accidentally exposing her vagina.

She was a singer, meaning, she sung songs into her body. Rubbing lotion on her skin seemingly took thirty minutes to an hour. She would sing songs to her body parts—thank her toes. She did the same thing with her grand-babies, and according to my sister, with me too. Before I realized that she was very different from other mums, I thought this was how all women "lotioned" themselves. Three days a week she would drag me to her aerobics class, my coloring book and crayons in tow. She told me once if you exercise, you could eat as much stew as you want.

My dad, born and raised in College Park, GA, tells everyone the story of how he met my mum in Nigeria. She was demonstrating an exercise to her friends who worked at the market. He only saw her from behind but he could tell that she was pushing her breasts up in the air. He said he was seemingly the only person staring in confusion. She wasn't like most Nigerian mums either, and folks just got used to that about her.

My mum, Miriam (Mary), was surely a Goddess and loved herself fiercely. While she didn't have the language to say so, she had this deep awareness of her body, even her stride ... she knew that her body deserved to be honored and praised ... even sung to. I am just like Mum. Can you believe it? Just like her.

Mum and me: A story about
lotion, breasts, and awareness

Thank you Mum. I love you so much.

DON'T BE AFRAID TO WALK LIKE YOU HAVE REALLY GOOD PUSSY. SIT ON TOP OF THAT POWERFUL VIBRATION AND LET IT MAKE YOU HAVE AN INVOLUNTARY REACTION, PERHAPS A SMILE. JUST GET THAT FIERCE FEELING INTO YOUR CELLS. DON'T WALK LIKE A REPRESSED AMERICAN. WALK WITH YOUR ASS OUT. DANCING HIPS. BE IN CLEAR COMMUNICATION WITH YOUR SPINE. BACK STRAIGHT. HAVE PURPOSE. RELAX, YOU CREATED EVERYTHING.

XC

HAVE YOU EVER HEARD THE SOUND OF SILENCE? I WOKE UP IN FERTILE SOIL, UP HIGH, IN A CATHEDRAL ECO-FANTASTIC HOME. TWO OF THE FLYEST MAGNETIC WOMEN OCCUPYING SPACE AROUND ME. AS USUAL I AM THE FIRST PERSON TO RISE FOR THE DAY.
I took a *cold shower* to tighten my pores and pussy.

I ate fruit, *seeds included.* I *slapped my ass to wake up my root chakra, pushed* opened the front door that had been unlocked all night, and I hopped out of the house like a unfazed deer. Pranced my lil round self on the mounds of earth. Not a vehicle in sight. I felt like I was dissolving into a spinning vortex. The haze. With my confused brain recalling city life, I wiggled my ears. The sound ... of ... silence. Hollow. Empty. What to do but to invite all the cool morning into me, I am so worthy of that afterglow.

All day long. In a temple. An Ayahuasca Temple.

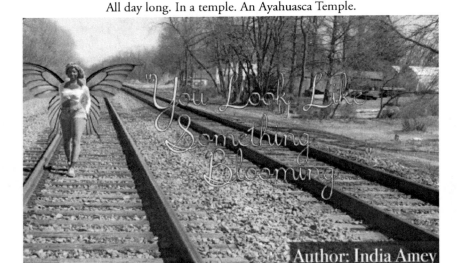

Photo by SenseThePoint

XCI

Your heart rate increases. Pupils dilate. Body temperature rises. Blood redirects to your legs. Cerebellum becomes more active. Brain flushes with pleasurable chemicals. A tingly chill twirls up your spine.

Whether with another person, a delectable meal, the enchanting ocean, a tree, or a bass line, you are deep inside the lovemaking.

Blooming Tip

Most things and eventually all things should feel like lovemaking.

"Storing healing memories inside my organs. It's an intense undertaking. Smiling profusely on the inside."-- India Ame'ye, Author "You Look Like Something Blooming"

Everything that happens in life is only given meaning by you, and whatever meaning you give it is taken into your body, more specifically into your organs, only to influence your entire (organ)ism and reconfigure every body system within (to support love or dis-ease). That's the science behind cancer, heart dis-ease, colds, and the like. Oh yum, now we can heal ourselves by understanding the brilliancy of energy and how it instructs ALL matter to move in certain directions.

I love being a spirit inside one of these human body temples, manipulating magic, merging with the stars, shooting miracles out of my body parts with just the simplicity of my left in-step. What we do daily is called magic, dammit. We all are sweet magicians, even if we have no idea that we are. Justa tossin' and turnin' energy around. flip floppin'. throwin' it back on all fours in wild, ambient trance. Abracadabra: not just words, but a way of life and Goddess knows I am just turning my lil self on...and on. Relaxxx saints, being easily turned on just means one's heart is wide open and readily able to feel deeply into a starburst of sensations. *shutters*

XCII

Wild passionate sweetness magic honey movement balance multidimensional healthy aura trance chakras bursting transformation abundance healing synchronicity nature water at least 7 OR MORE senses engaged to produce all sorts of minerals vitamins and pleasurable chemicals in the body temple for healing: Consider what happens to the planet if ALL lovemaking carried an element of Oshun, Lakshmi, or any other Love Goddess to it.

Blooming Tip

Dare to possess a deity during lovemaking and honor your lover as the God and/or Goddess that she/he is.

It was during a night of lovemaking that I merged with the Darkness. I accessed my Dark Goddess. The Emerging of my Whole fertile Self. My womb magic. The well water of spells and incantations. Opened my big ol' legs and gushed out fleshy old stories out of the *hole of existence. I was always to afraid to claim the Darkness, believing that it made me "bad." But silly me, there's no bad or good, there's only perception and belief. The fragmented me followed my learnings and conditionings from society, family, and implantations passed down in the blood. Reseeding my worth and graces within my ocean spit. Or spirit. Macheted the cancer hurting the land. Holy water pours out of veins. Pregnant, protruding wombs. We are all rebirthing the human experience through the legs of one, two, or 1 billion, using our creative imaginations to stimulate new neural pathways. Infusions of cosmic information cummin' out of assholes. Rooted. Here. Hole. Whole. Balanced.

XCIII

I am an ocean,

in trance,

throat open,

sucking,

with tears

and wetness

and slush

and droplets of dreams...

everywhere.

Sipping tea..... These dreams have not been deferred.

(Know thyself without shame, fear, or insecurity). I have never been interested in being a traditional writer. I am Living Art by way of the writing experience. Show and tell. No theories allow. Bless be the eyes of the witnesses.

153

XCIV

As much as I adore
carving
my *red clay*
lapis toned
curvy body
on top
below
inside
alongside
another brown body
similar to mine,
like a mortar
grinding
rose hip seeds
in preparation
of red tea,
like the *earth penetrating*
a twirling root chakra
squirting liquid stars...
As much as I adore
singing praise-songs
'black is beautiful,'
cause shit—IT IS...
I wouldn't be free
nor divine
if I didn't admit
that skin
decomposes
in this life, only
to leave behind
what is real.
Ethnicity is an identity.
A learned way of being and existing.
Spirit is a continuum,
outlasting the constructs of identity.
Identity is an attachment, temporary passings and goings...

Spirit is free space to create.
I have a hard time
admitting
that.
But I
just
did.

I love being Black but I am not bound by it nor anything else...Lapis skin, boundless experiences.

Ass-hip ratio: Many women desire a small, flat stomach and nourishing hips and buttocks. The reality is that you can do all the crunches in the world and not lose your belly. In my personal training classes, one of first things they taught us was there is no such thing as spot reduction. Essentially that means if you lose weight in your belly, it's because you are losing weight all over. Now what you could do is incorporate aerobic exercises (jogging or swimming) with an isolated lower body strengthening and conditioning exercise program. I wouldn't recommend a waist cincher or anything of that nature, as I do believe the body needs to breathe in order to receive and a constricting, tight object around the waist/core/organ area could cause issues in the long-run.

XCV

Make fresh juice for someone you adore.

These breasts cast love spells. I programmed them that way.

BLOOMING TIP

She elongated her throat, sucked on some sun, and
healed in the illumination of her own moonlight.

The act of sucking exercises and revitalizes the throat and activates enzymes in the
mouth portal, aiding in overall healthy digestion. Taoist women considered sucking
as a sacred act into the fountain of youth. Less talking, analyzing, and theorizing
and more deep throat sucking please. When googling "sucking" the results were
more or less about dick-sucking. Sucking dick (in whatever way that looks like for
you) is delicious and nutritious, but you can also suck other body parts from ears to

tongues, fingers to clitorises, to necks to breasts, lips to bellies, and of course from the sun to the stars to cucumbers and ginger root. "I can't talk I'm in full throttle bliss from sucking on these stars." Deliriously choking and gagging on this here sun!! Get it?! Heal thyself: Allow more earth (body parts or nature) inside on the in-breath.

More throat orgasms please.....for the channelling of your own unique voice and communications that can only be brought forward through your mouth portal.

XCVI

When you say "yes" to grown ass love, to love out loud, like ... to really do that shit, you have no idea what you are getting yourself into. All your fears will undoubtedly show up in well-worn hooker boots like 'Halo Goddess, you ready for me? I am here to spank your curvy ass into the sweetest surrender.'

This world affirms quiet love, don't let folks all up in your personal business love, or don't tell folks at 'Whole Foods' how hard you just orgasmed-love. Of course all of these things I delightfully did and will continue to do with tremendous ease and pleasure...thank you very much. The grace in understanding that your greatest fears are also your greatest gifts, professionally wrapped in electric blue bows and stained handkerchiefs, glitter free of charge. **Deconstructing fears is the ultimate freedom** as you evolve and stretch in unimaginable and indescribable ways. For so damn long (like decades) I was terrified to *let love rip me open and have its way into my unique mystery, into the curvy stardust particles, those parts unmet by bone marrow*. To be present as I could be in my full feminine fire ... and besides that cashier at Whole Foods asked how my day was going. I was just being authentic about my powerful sexual experience.

Sometimes tears became orgasms as I gave myself full permission to exercise my muscle to *feel*. Sitting in the mystery of the unknown and listening to a different kind of wisdom ... has been valuable. It is a profound gift to yourself stretched out into the universe when you *honor the wisdom that shows up in who you are and how you love* ... or shit, or **how hard you came**. **Again the world needs this brand of healing.** Out loud. Proud. Grown.

 Grown Ass Loving | A Story

XCVII

She prepares her body, home, and life force in
anticipation for her lover's arrival.

Her lover doesn't simply enter her. Her lover merges with
the
Goddess divine within her.

On fire, charged up from the earth inside
her anus and out of her throat.
Her lover recognized her singing and came to her service.

Blooming Tip

Consider going into ritual BEFORE you are entered or
experienced by your lover. You can sing affirmations into
your body, such as "All sex has been healing and will
continue to heal me." or "My pussy is worthy of receiving
nourishment and pleasure." or "My breasts are alive and
bountiful and suckable and healthy." Witness how your
body contours and shapes itself based on the words you
sing into it. Witness your lover learning to touch your
body and induce deeper pleasure in whatever ways you
require.

XCVIII

Pussy is a wet sponge for emotions, often holding generations of pain and trauma. Going beyond clitoral orgasms into full body orgasmic awakenings requires a willingness to lose control.

to let go.

to hold your head back,

open your throat,

uninhibitedly moan,

scream,

cry,

and shit.

Letting go: The Good Shit

———

Beloved, hit control, alt, delete on your belief. "You are not afraid of any aspect of Nature.

You are Nature. And there's nothing like looking into the eyes of a deer or fox in reflection.

As she walks through the tall plants, the pillars of initiation that grew from rich black soil, she stops every few steps to bask in the wonders of the world made manifest. With her throat exposed, she potently speaks in her native tongue narratives to plants about their inexhaustible power. A power that gives unassisted birth to the overwhelming living presence of love gushing into the world in uninterrupted streams. Halos of light surround her curvy dimensions, flooding her sweaty, 90-degree breasts with hazy memories on top of sharp realizations. "I have been here before," she moans. She, the Black Madonna on the cathedral wall, the dark core of the galaxy, the Mary Magdalene of Alkebulon, the fan and the peacock feathers, the nectar of warmth and compassion, the lineages of ancestors returned, the awakened prayers and sweetest liberation, the oceans and seas, growing food while sauntering into her next harmonious step. Servicing the collective's nourishment. Disservicing distractions. Barefoot and pregnant with ancient dreams.

XCIX

She straddles his lap ... facing him,

slides down her shimmering lace top,

and dares her lover to resist the

abundance pointing directly at him.

A feminine-embodied woman guides her lover into abundance by coming alive inside her body temple that has been **nourished and nurtured for abundance**. A woman assists her lover in becoming wealthier when she owns that the very nature of her healthy existence is total wealth and absolute abundance. She knows that every brand of abundance flows through her warm river waters. But no one can tell her that, she's just got to know for herself without worry, care, or concern for anything else (at that time). Since tapping into my feminine magic five years ago, every lover I have ever encountered finances/successes increased when we made love. The abundance resides within one's capacity to access it through being receptive to the energy of abundance and available to being utilized in this sacred way. Oh how dare I honor my powers out loud... Visualize abundance and tune inward into your body. Visualize an abundant body then insert yourself into the visions.

ABUNDANT EARTH BODY

C

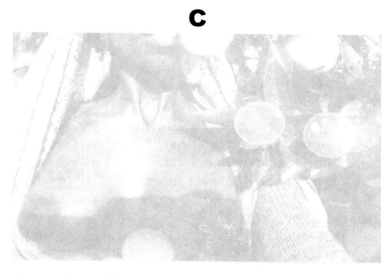

Consider not allowing life experiences to harden your heart (block your heart) which will harden (desensitize) your glorious breasts. Move through being emotionally hurt by people, by jobs, by experiences, and trust yourself to heal those wounds. Make small and large strives to get to a sacred place of power in how you process life, a space that that doesn't tax your body so harshly. Breasts are greatly sensitive to how you love yourself and love others. While my beloved birth mum was diagnosed with breast cancer, what she really should have been diagnosed with was a broken heart....*that never recovered*. Doctors will never ask you how you are loving, if you are hurting in your heart, yet the heart sits between your glorious breasts, so anything that happens to your heart will translate in your breast tissue. *Massage and love on your breasts outside the context of another person.* Let your own touch make you smile and get 'giddy.' Forgive people as you massage your breasts...*Goddess, just set those toxins free through forgiveness; Give them permission to simply leave your body through your nipples.* Pinch your highness (and your hardness) as you clinch your yoni muscles to unearth your divine sensitivity, one of the gateways to deeper feeling inside your mystery. Promise me Beloved, no more harsh self-talk about those *powerlines to the divine.* When your breasts are being wonderfully and brilliantly sucked, see them as extending nourishment like fleshy vitamins, because they are doing just that. Eat more green foods, practice divine acceptance, and give hugs with fierceness. Ahhh *yes darlin,' mouth ajar, throat open, lips protruding, nostrils open, gone into the meditative peace without fear, shame, or guilt.* **This is what healing looks like sometimes.**

When it's all said and done, all sex was love or a call for more love, even pain is merely a call for greater love.

CI

It's so auspicious that during orgasm your *thinking stops* and the only thing you are capable of doing is **_feeling_**. The more you allow your orgasm to permeate your entire body *(not just your genitalia)* the more you can actualize a life where **_ecstasy becomes a very natural state of being_**. The key is to reach for the orgasm *outside* of the bedroom in nearly everything you do thereby cumming in the bedroom becomes as simple and easy as blowing on dandelion and making a wish. It's your command, darlin'.

How to actualize an orgasmic life

C2

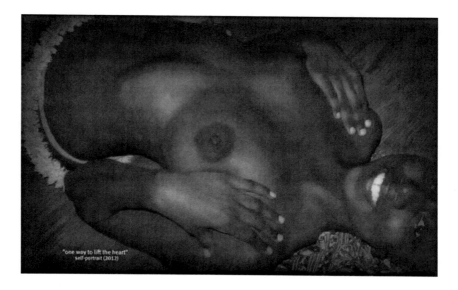

"one way to lift the heart"
self-portrait (2012)

The best way to shift your mood is to literally lift your heart. Lie back with your chest open (surrender position). Rub your breasts in circular motions towards your heart. Mold your body shape with your fingertips. Visualize your heart opening and radiating in every area of your body and shooting out into the Earth. Let love drip out the corners of your mouth, shoot out of your nostrils, penetrate your ears, saturate your throat, drizzle down your spine, and fill out your curves.

Become sci-fi, leave your body, then burst
into love's flame.

Beloved, are you more committed to your anger than you are to your dreams and pleasures? Observe what happens when you in all your receptivity call upon the passions never expressed. Ignite the bouquets of flowers along your spine. Don't judge anything, just observe.

CIII

I ONLY BELIEVE **IN** EUPHORIA,
IN ECSTASY, **IN** INTOXICATION.
IN BEING NAKED
ON MONDAY MORNINGS.
WITH MY TILTED HEAD BACK.
THROAT WIDE OPEN.
AGAINST ALL ODDS.
INSIDE MY DEVOTION TO PLEASURE.

 MONDAY MORNING DEVOTION

Consider writing your Monday morning devotion.
Sing/shout/harmonize your devotion into nature, even if only the plant sitting in your kitchen window. Nature carries that vibration into the soil of the abundant earth to distribute your dreams and goals wildly and freely and richly and abundantly.

—

Beloved are you cummin' and calling yourself alive too?

CIV

Ever considered moaning rituals?

Moan because your pancake turned out beautifully...

Moan because you stood up for self...

Moan because you trusted the process of life ... AND you made it through...

Moan because your green juice is clearing up your skin...

Moan because your right leg doesn't hurt as much...

Moan because you woke up with

a deep throat, a clean tongue, and clear air

to do so!

moaning ritual

CV

Your task is to shift intimacy and sex

into otherworldly dimensions.

First consider releasing your thoughts

about what you (have been programmed to)

believe is possible and uninhibitedly encounter

the impossible.

Otherworldly sex and intimacy

CVI

The only garments she wears at home

are ankle bells and waist beads.

She loves wearing sound. Being musical.

Even when she is far, far away,

her lover can't help but to get rock hard

to the sound of ... wind chimes.

A Story about Wind Chimes (sort of) | Music holds Memory

CVII

Breast massages accompanied by drinking lots of water offer natural cures for depression.

Breast massages circulate stagnant energy, hormones, pleasurable chemicals, and charged lymph fluid throughout your body, up into your heart and throat, so that you are not only CAPABLE OF FEELING love, you are also empowered to speak love into existence without worry, shame, or fear.

CVIII

Whatever you focus on grows

like lavender wildflowers in the soil (soul)

of your receptive body temple.

So consider watering your body,

becoming more juicy,

and courageously growing more love.

Then sit back and witness that man or woman

lose his or her mind, heal, and transform

simply because

he or she is inside the ocean of you

Lost in Oceania:
The Transformative Power of
Becoming More Juicy

…..She stopped looking for lovers who will not hurt her and instead visualized beautiful people who adored taking care of themselves. If one takes care of self and realizes self in others and others in self, then we are connected to do neither any harm.

CIX

GROWING UP *I* FELT LIKE GIVING HEAD TO BOYS WAS DISGUSTING SO *I* DIDN'T DO IT UNTIL *I* WAS 22 YEARS OLD AND SURE ENOUGH IT WAS THE MOST DISGUSTING THING EVER. NOW *I* KNOW IT'S BECAUSE *I* WAS NOT DEEPLY ATTRACTED DEEPLY AND INTENSELY ATTRACTED TO MY EX-FIANCÉ, IN A WAY THAT HE COULD BECOME MY HEALER WHEN NEAR, INSIDE, BELOW, OR OVER MY BODY TEMPLE. HOW APPROPRIATE THAT *I* WOULD ATTRACT A MAN THAT *I* WASN'T ATTRACTED IN ORDER TO SUPPORT THE UNHEALED PAIN AND SUFFERING *I* CARRIED IN MY BODY FROM STORIES *I* HEARD IN MY YOUTH ABOUT MEN, LOVE, RELATIONSHIPS, ETC. STORIES THAT NOT ONLY MADE SEX WITH MEN PAINFUL, BUT ALSO REDUCED AND PRETTY MUCH ELIMINATED MY ATTRACTION TO MEN.

When you start rewriting your stories, everything you know about yourself shifts. Your cells hear your new stories as you recite them over and over again and recalibrate to align with the frequency of the stories. You are free to tap into who you know yourself to be beyond the stories you heard and encountered growing up.

I had no idea that rewriting my stories would bloom my attraction to men again. I never even considered the possibility of that happening. When you ask for more abundance and rewrite stories around abundance, you will get more … more … more. And more abundant includes men and women, and excludes anything out of alignment with love.

Rewriting stories

CX

I met a lover in the most pleasurable summer I have ever encountered, and fell madly, wildly, and uninhibitedly into my attraction of him. I was reframing stories and transforming my life, and receiving penis again with an unprecedented intense rapturous, mutual attraction. Long and wild story short, I asked him if I could suck his dick one full moon night when things were so chill yet awkward between us. I was so shocked when I asked him, the 'good girl' image I grew up with was being challenged and shattering before eyes. I thought long and hard (surely no pun intended) about the visual of doing it to him, and when he said 'yes,' I pulled my hair up in a pony tail, laid back, guided him over me, and inserted him into my mouth. It was the most amazing feeling ever. I felt nothing but pure joy and pleasure in nourishing him with my mouth so much so tears that started streaming down my face. When that happened, he lost his composure and left an enormous amount of cum inside me as a result. I was gagging, spitting, losing my 'mind' and gaining and earning life force —all sacred actions of the mucous membranes realness.

The beauty of having a throat is that sometimes you choke, and the beauty of having a mouth is sometimes you spit ... beautifully delightfully choke and spitting action are amazing when you are being pleasured in the mouth with a healing wand owned and operated by someone you wildly adore, and I do mean ... deeply ... adore.

Tears of Joy and Deep Adoration

Blooming Tip
Rejoice in the bodily fluids of your lover. Oy!

CXI

Don't text a person for a response, **text a person as conduit of love**. Text a person to experience your gift and freedom *to be released from outcomes and surrendered as a feminine archetype* to the present moment, to give curvy movement to your throat chakra through words and intention, to engage pleasurable emotion in that texting moment. Whether the person responds or not is irrelevant to the experience you have just created for yourself.

Texting Freedom: Conduit of love

CXII

Just because you are sitting with sexual energy in your body temple, even if you are connected to a person in that moment, doesn't mean that the energy has to be organized and directed into a sexual experience. Sexual energy is the most potent energy on the planet—it creates and BRINGS life to everything. You can allow that energy to run wild, shake open your chakra fruits (healing your organs), and spill just a little bit of juice everywhere. That's your power and gift to yourself and the world. Consider the desire to cultivate your sexual energy inside and outside the context of another person. Because it's more than just sex; it's potent life force sipping. It means that your body is alive and activated and healthy and free to create.

CXIII

I am emotionally authentic and available. Sometimes I'm wild and free; sometimes I'm reserved and quiet. At this moment I am radically aroused, feeling the residual of that arousal overflowing into my creativity. I am not ashamed of pleasure as it brings forth tremendous arousal. My loose and free body moves to a rhythm of its own, incapable of being tamed, like my natural tightly curled hair in braids. Pleasure produces chemicals that heal my body; pleasure brings harmony to my cells, tissues, and organs. Pleasure allows me to go into trance and remember the ancient ways of creating more abundance into my life ... and into the lives of others, like community. Therefore I am not ashamed of my need to be pleasured or desire to give uninhibited pleasure often. ***Excuse me, but pleasure is the reason I don't have to take medicine!*** **All that** potential and prosperity within two undernourished egos and four rotating hips or in the willing phallus of an oak tree. I am grateful that my body is alive, exfoliating layers of repression, guilt, and insecurities. My heart is the open sky, and I feel the breeze serenading me with every breath I take. Being courageous enough to 'feel' is a gateway to healing, and all day long, I'm feeling—something.

You ever spend a whole day twirling??

 Emotional honesty and pleasure intersections

CXIV

An orgasm is NOT rooted in your genitalia. An orgasm is your very natural state of being. It's your personal freedom and ecstasy at any moment.

AHHHH spent three hours twirling in nature, deeply aired out *giggles*. This is the divine moment captured right before I went into trance and ceremony. Ahhhhh truly adore every bit and crevice of my body temple and the safety and pleasure and healing it brings me.

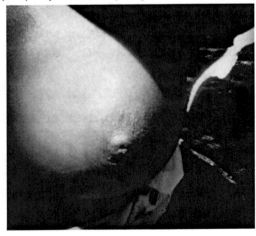

Got local honey?

174

I'm feeling......not doing. It's a process to allow oneself to "feel" without judgements because I, like the rest the world, have been taught to categorize emotions as "good" or "bad." Can you imagine the pressure one places upon herself to have so-called "good" emotions only? Giving myself full permission to feel, to experience every emotion deeply, during the 6-8 days before my moon cycle affirms me instead of trying to resist an emotion that is as natural and valid as "happiness." And guess what, to have the most amazing healing sex, intimacy, and love connections, you need to be able to feel, and you can only feel what you AWARE of. When some experience feels uncomfortable, certainly that is not the time to shut down, as feeling and digging deeper into that experience is growth that I would have dodged had I ran from it. Like any cleanse, the stuff that comes out of my body seems to go back years until suddenly ...I realize that it has healed or at least moved into a healthier place, as in 'not being shut down or denied'. Feelings are connected to the sensual, the sensual is connected to the erotic, the erotic is connected to the sacral, the sacral houses the emotions and ALL is simply connected to the divine and delicious omnipresent spirit. In this watery space (flowing emotions/yoni/sensuality), everything comes alive from a stone to my gluten-free, homemade biscuits to my goddess-given pms-sadness. Deep sadness feels safe to show up, and comes with many bags packed since I suppose it knows I don't have any other PMS-visitors arriving. No cramps, no heavy bleeding, no aches, no short patience. I don't know if this deep sadness will ever be permanently done with me, but I do adore that I have become better with how I process it. Sadness tastes like honey and I truly absorb a lot of that, like sunlight!

Blooming Tip:

Rub your ass cheeks and repeat after me:

There's no division. It's about striving to be balanced (whole) within one's body, not fragmented or incomplete .....which provides medicine for the earth. Balance within a human body nourishes balance within the earth body- the oceans, lakes, rivers, trees, and full body ecology system.

CXV

Intimacy begins with

the courage to listen to yourself.

The willingness to

see, feel, express who you are

without compromise.

INTIMACY (Into-Me-I-See)

Blooming Tip

Consider creating your own feminine practice.
Oil-pulling your mouth portal first thing in the morning.
Drinking at least one glass of water with intention and purpose.
Days to meditate and sing songs to your inner Goddess and outer Divine Reflection.
Special days for 2 hour coconut milk and honey baths,
lavender facial steams, and reading books like "Tantric Orgasm for Women."
Days to nourish on chunks of papaya and recalibrate your digestion.
Nightly breast massages in circular motions to activate and heal breast tissue.
Days for wheatgrass enemas and vaginal steams.
Your children don't **belong** to you, they belong to universe. And they need you
healthy, your highest royal honor.
Consider hiring a baby sister, renting a hotel, and conjuring your practice.
Become your own devotee.
You'll be better that way.

You have the money; there's always enough; and you are so worthy
*....**but only if you believe you are.*** *Oh how lovely what one believes is heard in her*
own minds first before anyone else has to chance to receive and affirm those
projected quiet beliefs.

As a parental guardian for two years, I took that attitude into my organs often.

CXVI

Please,

Please,

Please,

No matter what,

Cultivate your ability to fuck like a God.

~Walk Like A Woman, Fuck Like A God~

Blooming Tip

"You make grown men swoon from the way look to the way you talk!"

Perhaps strangely, oddly—I never consider how men will respond or feel when I'm photographing myself or writing (expressing). I do this sacred work for the healing of women, so that women will have the energy, tools, and confidence to dig deeper into the feminine mysteries and access to a greater source of healing and tap into a wild, juicy, and courageous way of life. I work with the intimate arts so that feminine energy can be worshipped back into its wholeness, and harmony and balance can be restored into our lives, families, and communities.

Express yourself for you, not for the male gaze. It's Priestess Work of the Divine Arts, to allow some intensely sensual, healing, most loving spirit or energy is given permission to actualize itself through your whole being. That spirit or energy forever affirms your beauty, worth, and divinity.

Love is the only energy that heals. When I create, I add more love into my organs. More love gives rise to more healing. If I am healing, so are you. If you are healing, so am I. If women are healing, so is the Earth's collective, men included. Because every body (and every energy) comes through the living nature inside a woman. Men and women are unable to help themselves; humanity gets stimulated by a beautiful, bountiful, loving woman. *But the stimulation is the desire to return to the nourishment of the womb.* We desire to consciously and subconsciously go inside to rest, rejuvenate, and renew. And anyone can. Find your sister, find her womb, and if the harmony is right, rest inside her without shame, guilt, or any other brand of fear. The ocean needs more water.

CXVII

If you are truly living inside

a liberated body temple,

you won't let religion,

or sexuality

or even your ethnicity

interfere with your growth, expansion, or connection

to love and being loved by any energy.

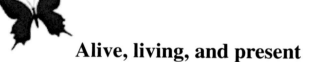

Alive, living, and present

Blooming Tip:

What I know is freedom is situating your life where working
for other people is only an option at best. Where loving, frequent
touch, playing in nature, growing your food, sharing meals,
preparing juices, enjoying music and the arts, and being fucked
until you fall asleep are uncompromisable daily necessities.
That's what I know.

CXVIII

Sugar cravings are purposeful. They indicate the desire and need for deeper intimacy, more specifically deeper layers of touch. Inside your pussy are meridians (chakra points,)that require stroking, massaging, balancing, and all manners of attention. When not honored, you will eat a whole cake as compensation.

Sweet tooth

Womb Freedom Love (Conjuring by way of the living-writing experience)

To access the mystical information inside your womb is to tap into your capacity to create more love in your abundant body, the collective body, and the earth body (all one in the same!). **And if you had your womb removed, please receive into your abundant body…that you don't have to a physical womb in order to connect with your (psychic) womb!! Beloved do you have courage?** Because it's the courage to allow yourself to spend large amounts of time with your legs open sans underwear, skirts, or pants. Allow your yoni to breathe in order to receive transformative (healing) information. It's such a natural high to live inside this full blown arousal, an indication that your body is alive and available to love and to be loved, to hold and to be held, as *touch* is the gateway to healing. The old southern churches I adore refer to that as "laying hands on" To have *knowledge* of healing and the courage to implement that healing knowledge into your daily life are two completely different things. I tell myself "*I don't just want it in my head, I want the knowledge and technology in my DNA, in every cell of my glorious being.*'" So I do my best to dedicate a certain amount of time to being my truest loving form incarnate, a Goddess of love, and breathing deeply through any discomforts, as all healing is simply the undoing of fear and fear is a way that people are controlled. As a result, all healing has to simply look like *love*, the grandest most royal decree of *freedom* for us **ALL. C'mon somebody!!**

SKIN-CARE/SKIN-HEALING BELLS Ding, ding, ding

You know when you make your loose leaf teas and you have an abundance (what a lush word) of tea granules and leaves left ever, use those tea particles in your scrub!! The skin is the most porous ORGAN in the body, so anything you put on your skin goes directly into your blood stream, mmm, what receptivity and alchemy. Mmhm.

Here's my favorite TEA-SKIN SCRUB. *Skin that's fine and delicate like soaked tea leaves.* **pardon me that was a line from my future commercial*** :)

Retrieve a quart glass jar, personally I love green glass jars....always activating my heart because there's no higher vibration than love and healing happens in the heart.

Burdock root (½ c) wet from water and steeped to perfection. It's ok to have some of tea inside it. All that tea juice share intimacy with your bloodstream. Throat open... (if the harmony's right, say "ahhhhhh")

Add to this love jar the steeped burdock + 1/4-1/2 c of an organic oil that offers your body the most nourishment (my personal favorite are sesame seed and jojoba oil combined) An aside about jojoba oil: it's the closest oil to your natural sebum oil secreted from your skin and hair, so your body tends to receive (there's that word again) the benefits more than other oils. Then add 1/2-3/4 c of himalayan sea salt. Then to activate my sensual charges, I add pink rose petals because ...again..worthy of being said again.... I love activating my heart. Place lid on top. Then shake. Not just with your arms but with your whole body...raise the jar to sky, sit it down on the earth and dance in your skin's royal delight and honor. Let stand for one hour in a cool place. If you use olive oil, place in refrigerator asap because olive has a low-heating point before it goes rancid. Not cute for the skin! After it sits, it's ready to be slathered on in the shower or tub. To preserve extra, keep in refrigerator for 3-5 days. If you add lemon or apple cider vinegar, it will last up to 10 days refrigerated. Learn your body's harmony and get that witch's bathroom apothecary in order for your beauty rituals. Relax Christians reading these words, a witch is just a healer, not the illusions projected on TV or in modern culture. Don't miss out on your unique brand of healing with herbs, thoughts, sex magick, and more. That's that witch's work and alchemy running in your veins.

CXIX

Sun. Planets. Moons. Are all Stars. Like You Are. When You. Orbit Love.

I love to ask myself "What is it that you need, love?" and delightfully fall into service by honoring my needs in that second ... in that opportune moment. On this day, it was a warm bath infused with rose petals and coconut milk, some dandelion tea, and a scalp massage. It was my moisturizing coconut scrub:

½ cup organic, unrefined coconut sugar + 1 tbsp of local honey + 1 tbsp fresh-squeezed orange juice. Mixed together in my special skin-healing wooden bowl. I love naming my "tools" and charging up their aliveness with my word-sound-powah. Prayed over then applied to my body by rubbing in circular motions. Circles represent wholeness as I touched my body back into wholeness.

How can I be of service ... to me?

CXX

*Don't be alarmed: I was having a bit of a
standing orgasm here. A woman easily excitable
is super orgasmic at any moment ... and
that pacific ocean was up inside me bursting
sensations into me.*

To preserve teeth and gum tissue: try OIL-PULLING

*Try oil-pulling1 tsp of sesame or coconut oil, swish around for 20 minutes or as
long as you can. Expel in toilet. Gently brush teeth for at least 5 minutes, 10
minutes is optimal. Please brush tongue. Make sure to release any mucous that
comes up from your throat. Get a new toothbrush at least every season, once a
month optimally.*

CXXI

Discover your brand

of enthusiasm and shameless joy

in sexually pleasing another

because that which you discover

undoubtedly discovers you.

~reciprocity

CXXII

Hard day at work?

Cum rest.

Inside me.

Enter into a soft night.

Tomorrow will be better.

~HARD DAYS, SOFT NIGHTS: FEMININE TALK

For all of the stay-at-home wives/lovers tending to house, doing yoga, making breakfast, dinner, and herbal teas, happily smiling and being naked, beautiful, and available when the Beloved walks through the front door...

This is Sacred Whore/ Priestess Work. Enjoy your journey into your Whoredom. First consider releasing everything you learned about Whores first. Deep breath yall :)!

CXXIII

WOMEN AND THESE BRILLIANT BODY TEMPLES THAT HOUSE OUR SOULS

I love promoting health, vitality, and well-being. I love giving side-eyes to repression, guilt and shame and adding more balance to the planet. Most mornings I look in the mirror without insecurity now, far different from just 4 years ago ... I love challenging old paradigms, constructing my body temple with my thoughts, and waking up to the freedom that my body knows it's adored and supported by its owner. **This is a divine right for everyone!** One of the ways to access health, vitality, and well-being is through finding creative ways to channel energy because stagnant energy is **impending illness**. It's simple: Everything that is alive has movement.

CXXIV

When struggling with something,

drink lots of water. Eat some sun with your *other* mouth (legs open please).

Engage your undulations

with ease and pleasure.

Soon the struggle uncoils from your spine,

releases into the earth, and liberates your entire body temple.

Oh!

~Snake medicine

CXXV

...Because. Every. Way.

She. Lays. Is. Wild. Activism.

~Pleasure Activist, Pleasure is w women's right movement too.

CXXVI

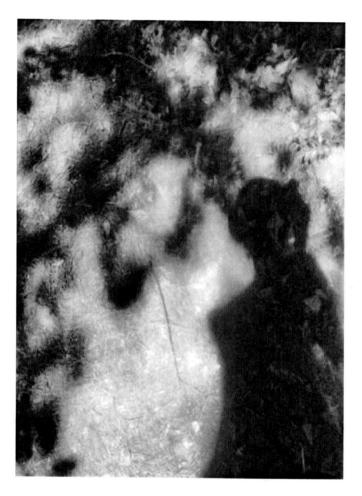

Shadows give so much away free of charge. They are not worried about money; they recognize what they will be replenished of their resources come noon. Here's my inner child showing up and clearing her throat chakra by singing to trees. How are y(our) tunes?

Blooming Tip:

My friend called and asked me to borrow $100, saying that she would repay me in August. I told her that I would give her the money under one condition. "Don't pay me back! We don't play those games here!" What I know about myself is that the universe is my bank and I'm always being repaid and supplied for everything I give, therefore I LOVE to give, as an abundant woman, with TOTAL EASE and GREAT PLEASURE! I have so much to give!

Plus there's always more from where that came from.

Get it? Ahhh, in-breath

CXXVII

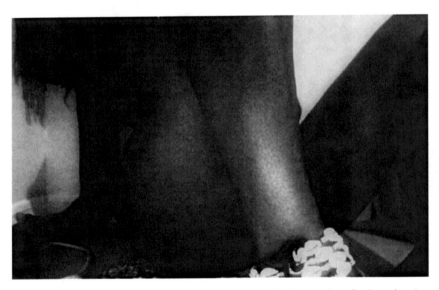

I am not a "nice" woman anymore because nice women usually fail to speak up for themselves. I advocate not being quiet, clothed, emotionless, or always on the bottom or in the dark during lovemaking. I advocate compassionate selfishness and clearing space for radical self-care and creativity stimuli. A woman who doesn't express herself suppresses the love, illumination, creativity, suppleness, and beauty of her spirit. Shout, moan, purr, curse, or pray. It's all the same thing: Manifestation now.

Loving, kind, thoughtful, nourishing, but not nice

CXXVIII

SECRETS TO FIRMING UP BREAST TISSUE

Now don't get it twisted, all breasts are beautiful and life-affirming upon sight, touch, or taste. I am so grateful for the existence of breasts. With that love considered here are simple rituals to lift, contour, and enhance breast tissues; some techniques I've incorporated on and off for the past 7 years. YAY for 7 year cycles!

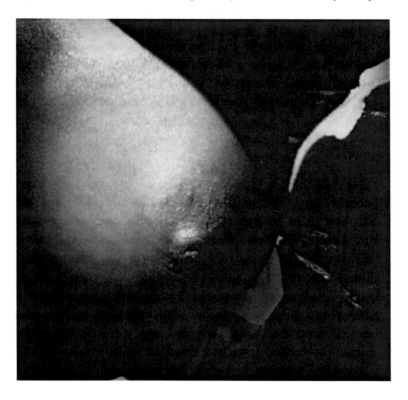

Fenugreek powder and capsules: Fenugreek firms and plumps up breast tissue and stimulate sensitivity and arousal which activates

the breast tissue. Use about 3 TBSPs of fenugreek powder mix with 1 TBSP of water and few drops of coconut oil. Rub the mixture onto your breasts in gentle circular motions towards your heart. Pinch your nipple during the rubbing. Let the experience bloom your arousal. Repeat for 5 minutes, 3 times a week. Incorporate fenugreek capsules into your daily meals. You should see results in 7-10 days! Continue for next 30 days! Observe your results.

Fennel seeds capsules: The high content of flavanoids in fennel seeds stimulate *tightness and add natural lift in breast tissue.* Follow instructions on supplement packaging. You could also drink fennel seed tea as well.

PLEASE NOTE

As with all herbal supplements, consult your doctor or holistic practitioner. I am not a doctor or herbalist and I assume no liability heretofore and afterwards. None of my aforementioned statements have been evaluated by the United States Food and Drug Administration.

Ok let's continue...

SELF-MASSAGE your breasts: Self-massaging my breasts has truly been my sweet secret to maintaining firm breast tissue at 38 years old. You want to move your breasts in circular motions towards your heart. Affirm the beauty of your breasts. Tell them what your desires are. Thank them for being of service. I love doing this first thing in the morning and/or right before bedtime. I make my own breast oil ('beautiful magnetic breasts' written on the bottle) from extra virgin olive oil infused with calendula oil, chamomile oil, broccoli seed oil, ylang ylang oil, rose otto, and frankincense. It smells like wealth I tell ya! You can make your own oil too but whatever you create, be sure it has calendula oil and chamomile oil as they stimulate breast activation and aliveness. Massage for 5 minutes! You've always had those power lines to the divine, now take action steps to assist them in coming alive. They have a lot of information inside to share with you and anyone worthy of connecting with them. Have a fabulous time!

_____Blooming Tip_____

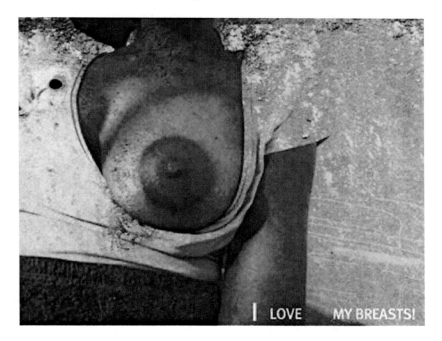

Most days I treat my body like a plant: Water, sunlight, loving touch, and communication are necessary for its health, radiance, and survival.

When you love your breasts, you subtly teach every woman and/or man who gets the honor to connect with them, how to heal them. Many times Goddesses don't even have to say what we need, we just hold the vision and intention within ourselves and take time to care for ourselves, and heal ourselves and others through intimacy and connection with others. That's alchemy and magic!

CXXIX

MY TOOTH REMINERALIZATION PARTY

I remineralized my tooth and this was celebration party. After being told that I needed a root canal, I went home and did my research on 'tooth remineralization.' I healed my tooth naturally by managing my stressors, as *stress will knock holes in your teeth*. Also I oil-pulled 5 times a week, supplemented with *fermented* cod liver and raw butter oil from Green Pastures online (that stuff is made of miracles), and added high doses of food-based buffered vitamin C tablets. Natural healing works wonders! This picture was taken after being cleared from my dentist that my tooth "grew" and no root canal was necessary. Of course! :)

CXXX

Even if a Goddess isn't interested in getting pregnant, she should still consider cultivating fertility within her body temple. A woman who lives inside a healthy fertile body is the ultimate embodiment of creativity, divinity, power, beauty, and magic. She carries within her an endless supply of vitamins, minerals, amino acids, probiotics, abundance, and magnetism. Where ever she goes, she attracts more love and light to replenish that which she shares with others. She walks the land, easily aroused by the wealth of pleasures of life. She is tickled by the mere sight of the sun or a frisbee-catching dog. People cross the street and stop their cars just to get a whiff of her fertility.

Fertile women smell like abundance AND the world simply can't get enough.

Blooming Tip

You can enhance your magic and magnetism through your word power sound: "I call upon all the passions never express by humanity to ignite within me now."

CXXXI

You're shaped like an unedited backwards letter 'S' from being (s)wollen with the (s)oaked mysteries of amber (s)unlight.

You were pre-ordained from birth in this twisted way. Numerous penetrable flowers bursting into a voodoo temple that makes a beloved cum way too quickly.

When the dark moon between your legs is on fire, decree the wind to blow up your curved spine and exit your protruding mouth. Engage your moans, wails, and screams as you arch into your next transition.

~1976 Year of the Dragon

Engage the animal spirit within. There is information for your healing, prosperity, and growth inside this frequency

CXXXII

I want to be so dedicated and devoted

to my femininity,

Where I am willing

and brave enough,

to create an abundant space,

for my lover

or lovers

to be "wrong,"

to make (so-called) mistakes,

and still be richly nurtured,

expansively held,

and generously supported

by me.

To feel unquestionably safe

to (so-called) FAIL,

And still be lavishly kissed

and flung into the land of tropical wonder

by me.

But first I must be committed to

creating that luxuriant space

for me.

Feminine devotee and proud

CXXXIII

STRESSED OUT? TAKE AN AIR BATH

I AM PICTURED AIRING OUT MY BODY TEMPLE IN 49 DEGREE WEATHER at SUNDOWN; A CLEANSE IN THE DEEPEST WAY. The cool soil between my toes extracted out energy unaligned with my thoughts, deeds, and actions. Do you know how much toxic energy gets trapped in the folds and joints of a woman's body temple? Did you know that the bottoms of your feet contain a roadmap to your organs? Touch your bare feet on the cool or wet Earth. Dig down into your soles to affirm your safety and stimulate your grounding. Get naked, out-of-doors, bend and contour your body in strange ways, and feel the gentle release in every cell of your being.

CXXXIV

Women should be watery like flowers.

Tears, sweat, and orgasms

daily. When serious activation is needed quickly, hourly.

Water bearers

CXXXV

Forget language.

Stretch your sound.

Test your voice.

Mmm, purr, and coo your way through the day.

Sing outside your register.

Exercise your throat to move sound.

Practice allowing sound to express itself

throughout your body.

Be willing to sound like a crow, a squeaky door, or a
wailing, ejaculating woman.

Trust the information encoded in your unique sound

to assist you in transforming your reality.

You may not be able to interpret the messages,

but trust the experience.

Then move out of the way,

and let sound do its work

without your judgments or concerns.

 Holy Sound

CXXXVI

Hymnals, medicine, elixirs,

galaxies, and other information

exist inside a woman's breasts.

When you are gifted the opportunity to suck,

lose your darn composure,

and act like it.

Suck or be sucked like the world doesn't owe you a single thing. Because really it doesn't. You birthed this world Beloved. You can help nourish its harmony as well. Your world. Your womb. Your nourishment. Integrated within the Hole of Existence. A container of the greatest power source on Earth: the power to create on all levels. So suck or be sucked. Possessed, amplified, and rippling in the highest honor.

Acts of service

CXXXVII

I figure if my spirit is inside a body temple, it might as well be inside a body temple that is alive and easily pleasured. Because of the aforementioned love, my body can come alive with the simplest of command. I am just that *please-able*. Here, here!

I take a machete to my trauma around "race" hence my reason for moving 3-6 months to Iowa and experiencing connection. More I am clearing my fears around having a child and acknowledging the spirit of the child moving in body and desiring to be of service to the world. I am clearing the fear of acknowledging my desires to have a family that includes a wife, a husband, and children. I clear my fears around unearthing my capacity to perform sexual body work as a Priestess of the Arts. I replace those fears with radical, sensual love for the reality that I am living in this moment, merging time, space, and physical dimensions through my visions, thoughts, speech, and actions. Affirming that is happening now, and so it is.

CXXXVIII

One of the reasons I love out loud from any and all angles through self-photography is because I love being aware of my body and the space it occupies. Am I hunching over? Can I sense my heart through my eyes? What are the hairs underneath my arms doing? What's being communicated in my eyes? How's my posture these days? Noticing my sacred lines and flaps of skin is having divine awareness of what is taking place within and around me. I especially love photographing my self from behind ... seeing the space my body occupies from the back. The full moon connected to my leg-limbs. I give myself full permission to be enchanted by the smallest of things I witness. It's not hard for me to do this; it's a **self-love ritual practice**, I suppose. Necessary. Purposeful even when it's not. Plus I really love myself when I am challenging my fears and doing things others may dare not to. At this point, I don't know any other way to live and truly FEEL alive and *safe*. It's also my way of giving thanks to a healthy body that is alive to the deliciousness of any slight sensation and stimuli.

 Photography as a self-love ritual practice

CXXXIX

Drink a liter of water then deep throat suck the masculine fire

from the earth's sunshine or another person.

In Preparation for Ecstasy

Blooming Tip

Go braless! Or at least limit how many hours a day you wear a bra. Bras restrict the flow of lymph fluid within breast tissue hindering the breast's natural cleansing process and stagnating (deadening) the energy in breast tissue. Anything that is stagnant is dead! If your breasts are heavy and ache, talk to the consciousness within your breast tissue, and tell it you are worthy of relief.

It could sound silly to some people to talk to their body parts. I try to step outside of what others think because for me it makes sense—plus I am living evidence of the great possibility of healing transformations amidst my healing journey. Every single body part is alive and like anything that has life, kind words are essential. If you need healing inside your breasts tissue, consider the healing formula may indeed rest inside you and the connection you have with the body temple housing your soul. Kind words, Beloved.

CXL

Women don't *always* need to speak. Sometimes we can just hang back in the wind and usher transformation in the silence because feminine magic blooms in mystery. Keep some mystery.

Silent transformation

CXLI

I haven't had a cold in 10 yrs or more and I attribute my immune health to healing teas. One of my favorites healing teas to prepare —especially during late winter/early Springtime- is nettles, pau d'arco, burdock root, astralagus bark, with a pinch of cayenne and turmeric, and dash of raw local honey. Add approximately 1 TBSP of all leaves and/or bark into a quart glass jar. Sit out under moonlight overnight. The moon generates more nourishment to the herbal concoction. Drink in next 4-6 hours or store in refrigerator for a maximum of 2 days. Research various barks, stems, leaves, roots, and powders and find the formulas that stimulate your blooming, Darlin'. :)

CXLII

When you start to ruminate in your mind, remember that whatever happens in your mind brilliantly translates into your body. If you are excessively thinking about what you don't have, fiercely interrupt your thoughts, like **"no!" or "cancel that!"** Begin to recite what you are grateful for, all the things that exist in your life right now. Feel that gratitude within and let it make you smile. Focusing on what you have places your body in harmonic frequency to attract more of whatever is NEEDED to sustain that specific frequency. Let ALL your wants/desires make you smile, excite you, and steam your arousal.

Here's an example of the automatic response of the body:

A woman pays for a trip to Brazil in advance and gets excited BEFORE the actual trip because she knows in a few months where she will be vacationing. She starts planning what she what will wear, special restaurants to visit, and the like. She gets excited; she smiles. Her body automatically responds this way because it believes that she is leaving. However it's not the money she paid for her trip with that made her smile, it's the <u>knowingness</u> that she is getting her desires met. Get it??

 Ruminate on your desires. Let them make you smile and steam your full spirit arousal.

CXLIII

Inhale the moon, exhale the stars. Matter follows mind.

A tip to juicily calm your body down

I live in a universe in which ANYTHING is possible through my thoughts, command, or deep-throat-purr with my head tilted backwards.

Heart and Throat Chakras Affirmations

CXLIV

One of the ways you can regulate your moon cycle is by giving attention to your aching uterus.

A visualization exercise

12 Tips to giving attention to your aching uterus

Drink a glass of moon-charged water (water that has sat outside overnight under the full or new moon) or red raspberry tea.

Relax into your silence.

Lie down with legs open.

Imagine yourself shrinking and shrinking and shrinking.

When you are tiny enough, see yourself climbing through the lips of your pussy—which means that you will have to know what YOUR pussy lips look like. Are they thin, thick, tight, loose, curled, wet, long, etc? Get a mirror and take your time.

Gently walk your tiny self through the entrance way of your pussy, as if you are walking through a sacred temple with your shoes off. Walk lightly and intentionally.

Gaze around. Breathe in and enjoy the smell. Feel blood fall like rain. It may be tempting to stop but keep walking. Enter the part of the temple that houses the cervix and uterus. Lie down inside the uterus.

Feel around. Massage your ailing parts. Ask questions like "How can I be of service?" Listen as long as you need to for answers.

Hum/sing/chant a song of gratitude for your uterus' truth, ease, and relaxation.

Visualize love filling up your uterus. Let this love make you smile.

When you are ready, allow the blood to transport you out of your uterus back towards your luscious lips. Exit your body. And with blood all over your tiny self, imagine becoming brighter and bigger again.

Bask in your experience. Tell another woman how she can soothe her uterus too.

 When you're ready, make time for your body. No one else can give you that gift. You can sooth your uterus if you just make time to do so. Less TV or social media perhaps?

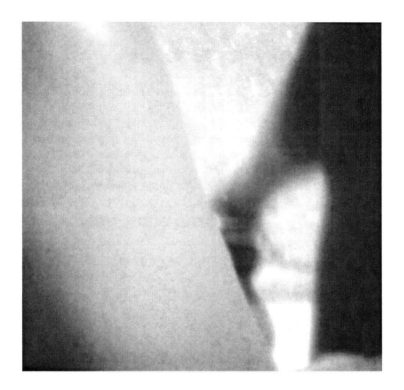

CXLV

No one ever expects you to not have panties on in a public park :) so it's very easy to let your yoni get sun-kissed during these times. Humanity is so busy being busy that in all the years of naked hiking, sunbathing, sun-kissing, air bathing, and just being naked or nearly naked in public parks, I have never once been caught with my titties or pussy out. I realized that once I shifted the idea that I could and would get caught into _I am safe, free, and supported in purpose and healing through the arms of divine love_. I signed my permission to be set free, nourished in my organs, and wild as the wind.

Expectations create reality

CXLVI

During my period of celibacy from other humans, I realized that celibacy can indeed be sexual. Because of my living, I am basically having sex all day long; I am aroused and excited by food, wind, people, conversation, laughter, trees, animals, and even my capacity to be clumsy and trip often. It's taking the orgasm out of my pussy and bringing it into my heart, where I am primed for penetration at any moment. Life experiences provide the harness for penetration and the electrical surges are redirected into my goals, dreams, and travels.

Sex Transmutation

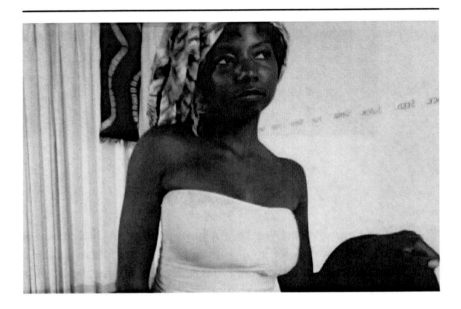

CXLVII

Don't you see how necessary it is for even grown folks to occasionally nurse on a woman's breast?! How this nourishment would atone for any depression or disease, essentially obliterating any feelings of being unloved or separate from the divine. If you recall, a person's feelings are the impetus to emotions and emotions have a great deal of impact on the body's ability to 'feel' or escape into numbness in preparation for depression, disease, and/or death.

CXLVIII

Don't play fair

Tinker with magic

Banish victimhood from within

Strive to be that good witch

Learn about herbs, roots, and flowers

Reclaim the ancient ways to give yourself an abortion

Know what potions and tonics to brew for illness prevention

Infuse your healing teas in glass jars as medicine

Learn sacred sounds and prayers

Bathe in the sun, the moon, the wind, the rivers, the rain, the soil, the trees, and the leaves

Remember how to heal your lover with your activated pussy hole(or any sacred body hole)

Celebrate your capacity to nurse grown people

Create your Bible of magic

If not, why are you here as a woman?

 Because women, at our best, are natural witches.

CXLIX

Women—stop depending on your lover for emotional support. Go to the waters of the ocean, a natural hot springs, a lake, or even your own bathtub infused with sea salt. Gather with other women friends. Make space to tend to women so that you can receive the same through osmosis and reflection. Consider not taxing your lover with your fleeting emotional and temper surges (as necessary as they are), let him/her be. Go to your friends, friends who are soft and yielding, the ones who hold the pails of water for you to purge into and can cool your head (and pussy) in a heartbeat. Feed oranges to the rivers, listen to messages from the ocean, have your friend wash your hair, or tend to you in whatever way you need assistance. Receive affirmations, herbs, songs, laughter, joy, crystals, incantations, and other gifts into your womb. Resolve love into ALL of life experiences-past and present. This will be an opportune time to reframe stories living inside your womb to a space that only love inhabits.

CXLL

You don't have to eat because you are hungry, you can eat because you love how food enhances the contours of your body. Do you *see* the difference word-alchemy makes...?

Blooming Tip

Reframe stories around food and the deliciousness contain therein. How you see food is how food interacts with your body temple.

———

CXLLI

...Because it ultimately comes down to choice, *remembering that we always have a choice*, therefore experiences are not just merely happening to us, they are happening through us, through what we create in our lives. Choice is a friendly reminder that any and all ways we move/bend/forward our lives are truly divine, appropriate, and necessary at that time. A Goddess never goes "wrong" this way. When you can honor that you are incapable of being wrong, you can relax and celebrate every choice that you have made to be where ever you are. *Every way that you are (and have been) is truly divine.*

CLII

court your breasts
be notorious about your power lines to the divine
advocate for their aliveness
massage them
with a special activation oil
'breast activation' written on the bottle.
move them in delirium
upwards and inwards in circular motions
get damp between the thighs because you are in your feelings ...
and it feels *good* to be feeling yourself.
rise in unconditional love with your bounty
just as they are
the consciousness inside your breast tissues needs that adoration
from you
in order to activate and transform.
When your lover touches them, she or he is indeed touching
Source and connecting to The Great Divine.

breast activation and transformation

CLIII

<u>*One of the keys to having an activated body*</u> is the ability to be fuck-able even when not necessarily fucking. To be sexy when washing dishes or doing homework. It's using your magical powers in mundane moments, where performing squat exercises resonates like *riding a penis* and eating papaya translates to *getting your pussy eaten out*. You feel everything deeply inside your organs yet you are unable to explain any of it.

Blooming Tip

Exercise in your home without clothes on. If possible, exercise outside. When you squat, slap your thighs and ass. Touch makes sound so h*ear* the sounds within. Let that sound excite your body and bring juice to your organs. When performing any chest or arm exercises, rub your breasts afterwards with emphasis on how you want your breasts to hang or rise. Intentional touch enhances your body's activation, a very similar way that sex does. The ass slaps, thigh slaps, and breast massages between exercises encourage your body to shape and contour in whatever way you that you want (and need). Your body is ready to recalibrate your figure as it is extremely activated thereby moldable like clay. You breathe deeply —up and down and your belly goes in and out as you are being penetrated from all angles by your very in-breath and out-breath. Simulating sex when exercising makes the body glow like sexual experiences enhance your magnetism. Ask me how I know?

CLIV

Lets get one thing straight: feminine energy is valuable and available to *all* beings. Whatever creates harmony in your body temple and environment is the energy that needs to be engaged at that time. Moreover feminine energy exists on a spectrum, not on some limited point and click binary, and can be thoroughly tapped into and activated especially in higher realms of existence: Goddess energy or the divine feminine. If not tapped into and activated, it becomes dormant, stale, and rotten. Think of the yielding, soft, calm, nourishing, warm, beauty, pleasant, destructive, fragrant, resting, at ease, stillness, passionate, creative energy and allow yourself to be held in these spaces. Wild and totally uninhibited abundance, like Mama (feminine) Earth, nourishing and nurturing the self and all of the vibrations (experiences, people, spaces) that the self encounters.

Feminine DNA | Earth

.....dream, feel, manifest your life.

CLV

Pussy is a wet sponge for emotions,
often holding generations of
pain and trauma.
going beyond clitoral orgasms
into full body orgasmic
awakenings
requires a willingness to
lose control.
to let go. to hold your head back,
open your throat,
uninhibitedly moan, scream, cry, and shit.

Full body awakenings

CLVI

Refuse to heat up your pussy, burst into flames, and create tumors inside your body (and inside the earth).

To de-stress:
Do absolutely nothing but receive.

A woman's (power). lies in the (soft space)

of her capacity. to be (stimulating and nourishing).

without trying to be. like warm (healing tea)

and (honey biscuits) made from scratch. just sitting there.
*(mesmerizing) anyone who encounters (her/them).*CLLVII

I am somewhere between crying and having an orgasm, metaphysically they are one in the same. Juicy women need to do these things daily. The world needs our brand of healing.

~Crying Orgasms Daily

CLVIII

In the morning,

add lemon + water + an intention into a clear class jar.

Drink your magic.

Slowly.

Slower.

As slow as you possibly can.

First things: **To wake up digestive system and manifestation powers**

Blooming tip (Shapeshifting)

There is so much gratitude that resides in my hips. Hips that have been nourished through kind touch, charged water, mugwort, himalayan sea salt, words of affirmation and loving language, prayers, commands and reprogrammings, candles, air baths, letting go and releases, breeze, wind, ocean, sunshine and rain, and delicious food and juices. I am so grateful that I was able to sift through all the bullshit in life and learn to love, honor, and adore my body for the beauty and brilliance it contains. Through those bit and pieces of connection, I also became aware of how eating certain foods, like local lard, an abundance of greens, papaya and cucumber, local raw milk-- country-girl foods-- **AND** *moving my body in high vibrational manners shifted the shape and contours of my body. Movements such as "tapping my booty" to invoke life and walking with purpose, feeling my hips when I move down the street. I also witnessed the transformations within my life and a shift in how the universe encountered me by simply being present with the power of command within my hips. How profound that indeed I have always been this powerful.*

CLIX

You can always ask for what you want,

even from your food. So

command your vittles to round out your hips,

soften your belly,

and heal your heart.

And know that it is done.

~Ask and *know* that it is done~

Blooming Tip

Tap into your brand of darkness. Essentially your balance and integrated wholeness. Get to know your shadow. Literally. At night make shapes with your shadows. In one breath you are exploring your magical powers to change the shape of your body and shift your lines and contours in various directions—getting sensually aware and comfortable with the power of your command in your body. In another breath, you are learning about your own beautiful darkness, the part of yourself you may not be aware of, but may seek out in the form of partnerships in order to experience a semblance of wholeness. For example, I have high attraction to mysterious people. Before tapping into my own mystery, I would to seek connections with people who were low-key, quiet, intense, but mighty powerful and present within their own energies. The more I dug into my own darkness, the more I realized that what I was seeking in my lovers was the experience with my WHOLE SELF. To experience my darkness and get turned on by the experience, meaning have a physiological response to my shadows. *Shadows desire to be noticed.*

CLX

Everyone comes to women—menfolks, womenfolks, and gender ambiguous folks. We are so watery when we are in our magic and power. That's the beauty and brilliance of femininity in a body that holds breasts and a womb space, in a body designed to nurture and create life and ideas. It's like going to the ocean when you lean on just one activated woman, BUT in order to be activated in this way, the woman has to be able to *receive from others, from herself, from nature and the cosmic collective*. When a woman can receive charges from the moon, she can activate all 37 trillion cells of her being and ONLY then can she HOLD space for others, including other women, without losing space for herself.

CLXI

Your body will shrink or expand according to how much you are being nourished or undernourished. Not just nourishment from food, but also from the willingness to be seen, heard, and supported. Receive compliments into your organs, loving and kindness gestures into your cells, and daily *coincidences* into your tissues.

Alkaline your body by ingesting the tendernesses of the day.

Fill up from love, allow the expansion, and take up far more space from being fed.

You can get a bigger ass (abundance) this way—*promise yourself* ... and live out the promise.

Variety of 'Food' for thought

Blooming Tip

When the body has been used for love, health and abundance are inevitable.

CLXII

How a woman receives anything in her mind becomes the root of her perception. That perception becomes her/his Goddess—meaning it informs her life, relationships, accesses, and successes. Check in on your receptions. Be aware of what you are receiving into your mind because ANYTHING you receive goes directly into your body temple and creates harm and dis-ease or nourishment and ease.

"Don't wait until you are sick to start nourishing and taking care of yourself" is my most reblogged post on Tumblr with over 18,000 notes and counting.

CLXIII

To be a woman is to feel electric and harness electricity into your body temple, the snake oil, the kundalini surge of your life force!!

Electricity from locally sourced vegetables—minimally processed foods, sunshine (little to no florescent lights), moonlight, nature, moon-charged water, red-clay body masks (literally red clay—i.e. deep dirt from the earth), wearing crystals inside your pussy (yoni egg), salt water baths, and the ability to feel the smallest of sensations like the caress of wind and of course larger sensations like full body orgasms contribute to electricity in a woman's body temple and aids in her manifestation powers.

Blooming Tip

Pay attention to what your spine communicates.

Just for this week focus on adding more light inside your body temple, chart your results.

Notice how much your spine straightens.

Infused so many stars inside my organs that the only thing that can touch me is love. Everything else...just misses.

CLXIV

Can you accept compliments?
Like deeply into your cells,
without feeling embarrassed or ashamed...
What a gift to be seen as beautiful in eyes of a human spirit?!
Worthy of being adored for your unique *gifts*...

Don't deny others the *honor*
of exploring *God* in a short dress
and giving her all the glory and praise
she deserves even as she crosses the street.
Through you.

~Compliments from God to God

Blooming Tip

Wearing strings, charms, loops, circular objects, waistbeads or body chains instantly makes your waist smaller. I'm not even considering physically, I mean metaphysically. There's a metaphysical component to any and all things physical that informs a healthy body among many many other things. The physical is tasty, but I always begin my magic in the metaphysical realms first.

CLXV

If you make the sacred choice to remove any part of
your body for health reasons,
be in celebration about your decision. You are still whole and
enough.
You are desired and worthy. You are sexy and worship-able. You are
complete in your choices. You are orgasmic and can continue to
unravel your orgasm and feminine mysteries.
Removal of the physical doesn't impact the metaphysical.
Tap into your *psychic* womb or psychic breast energies for support.
Believe in the stars that you cannot see
and go deeper into what you can *feel*.

Mama Mary (Notations to countless of women who remove their breasts and wombs. Sacred feminine mysteries still lay inside the energetic space even when the physical isn't present. *Glory be to the Goddess who lives in us all.*

CLXVI

If you are eating, you must be releasing from your excretory system or shitting if you will. If you are not shitting, please stop eating and start juicing.

Because clear skin begins with impeccable digestion

CLXVII

Radical self care.

The beauty of self-care is that you don't need much of anything to do it! Take baths. Move your hips, consider doing squats just to activate your grounding and connection to your womb (the creative source) and the earth. Self-massage your breasts. Eat colorfully. Drink water infused with lemon, lime, ginger, and/or grapefruit. Hunch on some sun. And be radically gentle with yourself. These are some ways you invite your Goddess spirit to rise and shine in your life and in the life of anyone who encounters you. And always be deliriously proud of yourself—even if you're simply laying in the bed and snacking on a bag of chips :)—be proud! You are so worthy of having snacks in bed, you see!

Simple ways to love thy self

Blooming Tip

When I don't like where I am in life and love, I inhale my roots from the earth and exhale my surrender, then simply move on.

CLXVII

A friend and I massaged each other's breasts with natural black sand from a California beach outside of Arcata. Sisters (meaning women of ALL ethnicities) — consider helping one another's kundalini energies to rise and hearts to open. When you help another woman heal, you are also participating in your own healing.

Simply if she is healing, so are you.

The surge of energy from receiving touch is one way to activate the body and create transformation and change into lives and communities. Be fiery and *FREE FROM LACK* OF TOUCH (one of the unspoken impetuses to disease in the body). Touch your sister as your lover— the details of what happened are inconsequential. Moan, purr, or growl in royal delight.

 Just love her, touch her, and help her heal. Witness transformation in the lives of everyone involved.

CLVIX

Vulnerability is the

impetus to true intimacy.

when a lover

is unable to be vulnerable,

spaces in the body are abandoned;

crevices left untouched, unhealed, and unloved.

mold grows and

the body dies.

~Metastasis~

CLXX

If you can imagine yourself under a waterfall in Peru,
you will immediately be transported to a waterfall in Peru *within
your energy system.*
The body doesn't know the difference between the actual and the
imagined.
It just surrenders to whatever the mind says or does.
So when you drink water
allow that water to evolve into a waterfall.
Go to Peru on your lunch break
and when you come back, you will be grounded and cleared.
Charged and rejuvenated. Armed with visions and dangerous to the
capitalist structure,
because you know at any breath
you are free to travel to Peru again without spending a dime.

UNIVERSAL EXPATRIATISM

CLXXI

Be a clear body of water
releasing juicy waves of ecstasy
onto everyone
and
everything around you.
Feel the arousal that something wonderful is happening
to you today.
Honor your healing powers to spray life into everything around
you.

Are you soaked stuff up yet?

**Women are watery and contagious when liberated in our body
temples**

You may be reading some of my words thinking "Is she for real? Can my body feel like a living flower? How? I work. I go to school. I take care of babies. And the reality is that if you do any of those things you have to consider having structure to your life—being ghost from the activities of the world to work on your healing. Less online, less going out, less aimless smoking, or anything that takes your "time" away. Go away when you're off from work and be steadfast in implementing transformation.

CLXXII

Get angry
but don't allow anger to
ferment, metastasize,
and invade your organs.
Allow anger to be massaged
out of your erect nipples
while supine into a watery mouth,
the warmest transformation of love.

Breast health care plan

CLXXIII

I.

She was prone and present,
in silence and orgasmic bliss.
Charged up magnetic crop circles for breasts,
larger from additions of moonlight.
A wild and blooming body temple
changing the shape of proteins,
reprogramming structures of DNA,
re-triggering pleasure hormones,
shapeshifting patterns,
in and out of trance to access shamed grandmamas,
but accessing her grandmamas was accessing herself.
Liberated and exposed in her relaxed, saturated throat.
Every way she laid is wild activism.

II.

Activism is the uninhibited ability to nurture and support the body
and all the ways in which the body responds are transformations.

III.

The illusion of time broken inside yesterday's pleasure.
Your healing is grandmama's healing.

Reframing stories: How reframing changes perceptions and *new* perceptions influence reality

CLXXIV

When I was depressed, my body looked depressed too. I felt weighted, like I was being dragged from my breasts down to my buttocks. That's why being in our pleasure is so essential. I don't care if you are an accountant or a single mother of a two year old. Being in your pleasure truly is power and at some point should be your #1 priority. When you're in your pleasure, life translates in healthier ways, as your pleasure is your magnet to your abundant points of attraction. The ability to feel turned on from the simplest of things when no one is present but you is **being** *in your pleasure. Feeling the littlest of things and allowing those things to make you smile. Coming alive, like actually cumming ... alive ... even when nothing's really going on, but you feel amazing over that nothingness, like being "IN LOVE" ... that juicy hormonal bonding feeling that you can relate to even when washing dishes. Then consider how expressing adoration for your body temple is the healing.*

My breasts know how much I adore them. I have been telling them so since I was 16. I am always massaging them and enhance the natural sensitivity in my body. They rest in salute over my praises and **nourish me first** *before nourishing my lover, partner, friend, or strangers from the smallest sight of them. Any potential ailments or cancer cells cannot exist under that awareness and conditions.*

Allow your breasts to nourish you first. And witness their transformations.

CLXXV

True sisterhood is where we are free to reveal ourselves, basking in each other's genius and beauty. Not so quick to *snap*, let go, blame and shame the other. We *can hold space* AND let sisters just be.

When you are loving your sister, you are consciously looking for the beauty and brilliancy in EVERY woman you see. You offer encouragement, respect, compassion, and understanding, even if you don't intellectually understand, you can *feel* her.

You can smile *into her*, knowing how deep conditioning operates, and love her no matter what she does or says. You know that you can drop to the place where you feel that She is just like you - vulnerable, unsure, longing for true connection, longing to be seen, known and appreciated in Her wholeness. You can smile at Her with your whole self, and your smile can say 'I see you, love. I am you in reflection.'

Sisterhood crosses ethnicities and cultures. Its truth is boundless and free from illusions of separation.

CLXXVI

Never stop moving. Anything that's truly alive has movement. Or it dies ... eventually. I love moving like a cat. Just moving with awareness of the royal energy I behold.

CLXXVII

Breast massages accompanied by drinking lots of water offer natural cures for depression. Breast massages circulate stagnant energy, hormones, pleasurable chemicals, and lymph fluid throughout your body, up into your heart and throat, so that a woman is not only CAPABLE OF FEELING love, but is also empowered to speak love into existence without worry, shame, or fear.

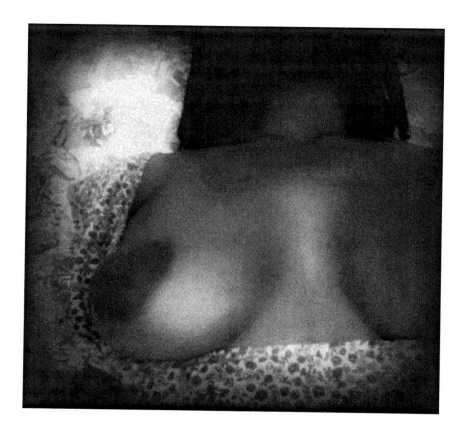

CLXXVIII

Pleasure principle:

Be wildly passionate
about something.

For me it's nature, photography, healthy foods, orgasmic living, minimalism, gardening, moving my body temple, bicycles, music, otherworldly sex, art, pleasure, abundance, healing, nature, loving, <u>and unearthing more ways to embody love in my cells</u>. *What are you most passionate about and how often do you experience your passions? It's most important that you experience your passions daily, but when under stress and desiring to gain a quick resolve and recovery, hourly.*

CLXXIX

The most loving and supple thing we can do for ourselves is surrender and honor other people's choices. The choices another person makes are neutral; our reaction to their choices only makes them either positive/negative, right/wrong….for us, not as a standard.

Our responses to the conditions and expectations we place upon others form patterns in our subconscious minds. **Did you know that the subconscious mind makes up about 85% of our brain?** Everything we see, hear and experience roots itself in the subconscious and those roots act as 'internal magnets,' attracting more of whatever we believe and receive as truth. *If we remember that our subconscious is composed of our past experiences, old thoughts, everything we've been taught about ourselves, then how we *learn* to react to other people's choices or how we react when others don't do what we think they should be doing, then we see our capacity and* **need** *to reprogram our minds…to rewrite the scripts we tell ourselves. We also see how it's never really about the "other" person —it's always about us as individuals, as we are creating everything around us, and seeing our reflections in our experiences with others. How cute!*

So lets begin with me and some fundamentals that I have imprinted upon my subconscious. Those fundamentals that have shifted my entire life to one of great abundance, wild pleasure, healing and transformation, beauty, self-responsibility and an intentional hourly bliss over seemingly ordinary occurrences.

'I desire not to be hurt by the actions of others; I desire to see others as healers and central to my healing experience. I honor a person's divine right to not do or act in ways that I deem appropriate or right/wrong.

I embody love in every area of my life to the best of my ability and celebrate my

236

capacity to flow through whatever shows up in my life through the lens of love.

No person, animal, or spirit desires to hurt me. No person, animal, or spirit is even capable of doing so. Everyone and everything I encounter is a reflection of me, a living goddess embodying love. That's the command I place upon life.

I am not at the mercy of the actions of others. I can be deliberate and intentional in my emotional response when I simply desire to do so.

<u>Oh Great Goddess as a Living Goddess flowing freely in my wild, childlike spirit, I dance with any fears that show up until I resolve them back to love. This sexy dance heals and re-programs my script.</u>

Feeling hurt, anger, sadness etc are emotional reactions to life and the behavior of others and we always have a choice in what emotion we choose to engage. We learn what emotion is "appropriate" to choose based upon our programming. For example, XYZ steals money from my bank account and I am now sad and hurt as a result. The action of stealing is neutral; the person can choose to feel sadness or hurt or surrender to what has happened and get to a place of acceptance, which eventually will happen, even if it takes 20 years or on one's deathbed—the beginnings of many people's deepest surrender. Acceptance is love. Accepting alleviates pain, hurt, and other forms of suffering. Acceptance is radical self-care. <u>Acceptance helps the body to enter into ORGASM!</u>

I can choose hurt, anger, or any other fear-based reactions if I desire to, but I make myself aware that it is a choice I'm making and when I'm ready, I can choose love. The sooner I choose love, all suffering of my mind, body, and spirit releases itself from my body. No more outsourcing my emotions onto others; I am responsible for my feelings and that responsibility enhances my magnetism in every cell of my being.

"Society has a tendency to solely congratulate the "doers". Sometimes this may make you feel like you're not ever doing enough. But "being" is far more valuable than "doing". If you're being a great mother, a great father, a great friend, or even just a great human being there doesn't need to be a validation from society or anyone for that matter-- in order to feel proud. You don't have to be perfect either....just strive to be your best."-India Ame'ye

CLXXX

Full Moon Intentional Barefoot Walk| A Meditation by India Ame'ye, Author

Purpose: To release anything from your body, mind, or heart that doesn't service your path.

The courage to release is actually an anti-aging modality. Simply put, all experiences that tax the body get stored into the body. Walking barefoot on the earth neutralizes any experience, past or present, that may be frustrating, ailing, weakening, or arresting you. Take off your shoes and feel into your senses. Amplify your body by feeling the temperature of the earth underneath your feet and walk with the intention of healing. Let the experience incite a reaction; personally I like to allow my experiences to make me smile. Perhaps you will have a different reaction in your body that works best for you. *And trust your movements....*try to move beyond any fears or hesitations to take the next step. Get it? Cheers, India <3

This meditation was given to me by the ancestors.

CLXXI

During hard times, rejoice in
the opportunity to minister to your spirit. Because
in all experiences, many celebrations live
somewhere within them.

Sometimes what believe is your weakness is really your strengthen turned inside
out, right side up, horizontally inverted.

So I accepted that I was an unconventional
writer...and then decided to publish my work.

CLXXXII

On Food

People always ask what I eat and to recommend diet programs to them. Here's my thoughts on food and why I don't recommend diets, but I do recommend *feeling*:

I don't eat McDonald's but I'm not "against" McDonald's or any other fast food places either. In some way being radically "against" anything is actually being "for" that thing you are against. I am more so aware of what my body's needs are and I trust any cravings that show up and the messages I receive from them. Sometimes I need nutrient dense juices, large bowls of local veggies, black rice, and herbal teas. Sometimes it's pound cake, sometimes it's lamb burgers, sometimes it's wild salmon, or just lemon water with added basil leaves —lots of it. (Basil is an herb that calms the spirit, sometimes referred to as "holy basil" in concentrated forms. When added to water, I refer to it as holy water). Sometimes over the top sugar cravings mean that I need a wheatgrass enema, more radical self care time in nature, and kind touch. I know what I'm attracted to — well-made ingredients, preferring coconut sugar over refined and processed white/brown sugar —but I am also flexible with homemade lemon pound cake prepared by friends or sweet older ladies with love. Sometimes I need very flavorful, savory, spicy dishes to activate my DNA, and sometimes I may want a fish sandwich from the *local Ma and Pop* restaurant. Much of my health has to do with having impeccable digestion by taking probiotics and eating in moderation. It's MOST important to love what I'm eating, and to simply enjoy my food, and bask in the varying textures, flavors, and colors as the juices touch my tongue and glide down my throat. To enjoy chopping ingredients and cooking. To enjoy the dining experience. To enjoy the aromas. To eat off real plates and make time for food presentation. If you truly enjoy McDonald's then it resonates at higher frequencies in the body than someone who's vegan and eats lots of vegan, soy meats to substitute for the McChicken's they still crave. Although there's so much information out there about how McDonald's is bad for the body, it will take a lot of internal effort and magic to maintain higher frequencies when eating it because the dominant collective thought is that McDonald's is "bad" food and that's how it resonates in the subconscious mind which influences your entire life. In fact, your current health and the condition of your body are outer reflections of your subconscious mind. The aforementioned is not in any way or effort to blame nor shame, but the sheer de-light and love to empower transformation (when you are ready). So whatever you eat, just enjoy it. *Sometimes it is as simple as less social media to put more time into food preparation.*

Take an air bath. To cleanse the largest organ of your body: the skin

An air bath. To cleanse and air out the largest organ in the body. But the greater truth is I just don't like wearing clothes. –India Ame'ye. Author. Kali. USA

and all the energy impurities it may contain.

Just get naked outside. And let your body move itself.

WHAT SEEDS DID YOU SOW INSIDE YOUR WOMB THIS SEASON?
Your womb is always fertile, ready, and available. Sometimes it requires rest and other times it requires activity. If your womb is ill or has been removed, tap into your psychic womb, the creative force that lives within. In a dark room, legs open, visualize space. Blackness. Cosmic Energy. A black hole. Oh Beloved—you are now seeing your whole self.

CLXXXIII

It's not only important to focus on the suffering, disparities, and transgressions women experience in society, but also on women's pleasure, wellness, and how we encounter, communicate with, and love those areas within ourselves and within each other.

Pleasure movement

CLXXXIV

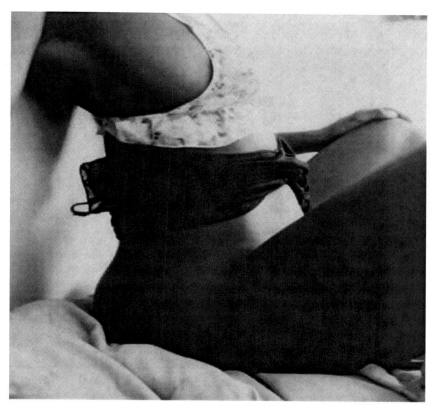

If I had children, they would *hear* me making love just like they would *hear* me doing anything else. From birth, they would hear my lover and me. They would know that lovemaking is a safe and loving experience shared between adults who love one another and they would hear my joy through my word/power/sound. They would see my afterglow, a reminder how sexual energy *heals organs*, including the skin, the largest organ, *revitalizes the heart*, and *makes every cell and tissue shine in delight*. It would be stored into their subconscious minds that sex doesn't *have* to take place in a dark room with the windows closed, with adults who are reserved and quiet, like they are doing something dirty or nasty or even unnatural. They would know sex is as natural as eating a tasty meal with someone you love and adore. They would know that their mama is a sexual being, and chooses freedom in her living. It would be so natural to them that would tell their friends not to worry and say "Oh that's just mommy crying. She's probably in her pleasure again with her love. Grownups do that. Lets go play board games." I would raise them this way *from the moment they were born. No sexual worries, shame, or fears.*

CLXXXV

Consider jogging in nature in a loose, short skirt and outdoor shoes. Don't worry —your pussy won't hang out. For years women exercised in dresses and skirts without issues or concerns.

Because active pussy needs to breathe in order to properly receive.

Also consider the illnesses and infections that harm the yoni portal can be attributed to lack of personal connection and lack of ... guess what ... *AIR!*

Rejoice in how nature cleanses and clears pussy in a way that soap and a rag are unable to. AND FREE OF CHARGE TOO!

She saunters into the room
not as a victim of the world,
not full of shame,
not insecure,
not doubtful,
not limited,
not poor,
not broken,
not heavy in her heart.
Only light on her feet,
navigating her fears,
communicating through her spine
as the indomitable and juicy presence of love.
Intentional in her choices,
Intentional in her language,
Intentional in her thinking,
Intentional in her creations,
and mighty intentional in her strut.

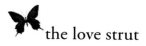the love strut

CLXXXVI

KNOW YOUR RIGHTS. It took time and observation to write these rights. What are yours?

1. I have a right to passionate love and wild ecstasy, to feel tipsy from drunken rapture and overflow in aliveness. I have a right to receive and give really amazing, transformative head. 2. I declare my right to feel extraordinary, free, capable, joyful, majestic, curious, abundant, beautiful, royal, richly refined—just as I am, in every way that I am, in every area of my life. 3. I have a right to cultivate my connection to Mother Nature, the Springtime that is happening inside my womb and celebrate the accompanying blooming creative actions. 4. I have a right to my pledge my allegiance to honoring my emotions—and honoring my ability to feel, be adored, . . . and receive pleasure inside those sacred emotions. 5. My womb is illuminating, transformative, and incapable of making mistakes therefore I have a right to believe that ALL sex, love, and connection—inside me, through me, around me, ancestral, alien, or otherwise, have been healing to me, purposeful, and for my highest good. 6. My body opens like wild earth, a paradise with big ol' brown legs-streaming magic and majesty and delirious enchantment. With that understanding, I have the right, once again, to receive really amazing head. 7. I am a transformative ocean and a mysterious vortex of cosmic construction and I have a right to walk and live as such. 8. My yoni is bursting into stars. I am ready to greet The Big Dipper again and I have a right to embody a legacy of kind touch. Some affirmations I recite (sometimes out loud and sometimes quietly) *before I am touched, kissed, or entered in any intimate capacity. Eventually the lover gets used to it.*giggles**

 # WHAT ARE YOUR RIGHTS? NAME THEM!

CLXXXVII

Oh Tomorrow, I love you

without knowing you ... yet

~The Metaphysics of Unconditional Love ~

CLXXXIII

I love you always without remaining bound. I am suspended between the past and this next letter I write in this journal. Perhaps it's the season that forces me to reflect, sometimes weep, but mostly celebrate my experiences swirling in the quiet night sky. To the land, to the stars that inhabit my body, to the sea, to this glass of water, to my favorite homemade biscuits, to the jasmine moon's invitation, to the children, to ancestors becoming lovers, to friends as lovers, to silver string connections, I honor you. I withdraw on tiptoes, without telling a soul, fleeing into the safety of wildness and freedom. Relationships are beautiful in their complexities ... and I love that we were both brave enough to love to the best of our abilities. And mmmm, didn't we love? Or was it really love? Did I love?

Love Check-Ins: **love** in practice and evolution: lovers, partners, and past lives

CLXXXIX

Courage to receive/feminine —presenting woman

To be alive in a luscious body is to receive sometimes or many, many times without worry, care, or concern. To experience the sensual (the senses), the kundalini fire or aliveness needed to heal and transform one's life can only happen when in energetic harmony and balance within the self. The inability to receive is a huge energetic block and energetic blocks are impetuses to greater dis-ease. It's something my mum, as beautiful as she was in her body temple, had a very difficult time doing. It's something that my sister and aunties had a hard time doing. It's something that a few of my past lovers had a hard time doing. Even women who are highly feminine -presenting have a hard time receiving. The guilt, shame, blame, and repression run deep in the cells, and the blood connects to the organs and informs the organ(ism) or human body. It's the nature of a society primed and pressed in monolithic thought and socialized to experience love as an outward manifestation instead of an internal state of being. The body loses its ability to feel and has to be overstimulated back into *marginally* feeling at best.

Blooming Tip
A massage is not about sexual gratification,
it is an offering to awaken your sensitivities and relaxation
chemicals and hormones
and help remove toxins and other blockages out of the body and
into the earth,
the warmest transformation of love.
Massage someone you love: a friend, coworker, neighbor,
clerk, or lover. An offering to the deity living within ALL. An act of
service to one's highest self.

CXC

Being brave enough (because it does take tremendous courage) to become an orgasmic women/women/a person with a yoni/goddess is learning to uproot and transform deeper hidden and sometimes not-so hidden (i.e. tumors, fibroids, heavy painful moon cycles) EMOTIONS in the body. The gateway to receptivity, pleasure, and any ability to rewire your neural network in an effort to create transformation and change in your life through your yoni/pussy/vagina but will be inaccessible when blocked by emotions that stress the body. When you are ready, you can stop trying to have an orgasm, and become the orgasm through your healing, living, and relating orgasmically and pleasurably to everything, all things (eating, cooking, cleaning, fixing your hair, etc.). You may stand out from most. I love being a soul inside this gorgeous body. Five years ago I took on the challenge of dealing with my pain surrounding my childhood, emotional and physical abuse, women, men, money, not having enough, not being enough ... and I am now here in the mist of a great clearing. Not perfection, but healing bit by bit.

The Great Clearing

CXCI

It's 348 pm ..and I am in pleasure while chopping red peppers for a Ghanian feast that I probably won't be able to eat since my pallet has changed. But I don't mind. Food prep is a sacred act ... turns me on actually, with my hard nipples and engorged clit. If you ask my internal organs right now, they would say I got my activated breasts out pointed at the Bahia sun, an expat eating local fruits and drinking something wet, sweet, and healthy just for the delight of my organs. Yea, it's 3:49 pm now ... and I am still in my
pleasure. My plumpish body is wildly alive and being pleasured by Ghanian rap music and cross-cultural chatterings.
I can't stop smiling;
I think the sun is stuck inside my mouth.
Everything word I speak sounds charming like love and the lusciousness of loving. Soon my mind will catch up with my body and remember I am merely cutting red peppers on an aged cutting board.
Yet I am the brilliance that lives divinely inside a human body temple. And I can't stop smiling.

3:48 PM-3:50 PM: 2 Minutes of Bliss

Blooming Tip

I am deeply sexual active! I get penetrated daily, mate! The ability to feel spirit is THE penetration! It goes inside! Church!

CXCII

Steps to leaving:

1. Get rid of your shit. 2. Go.

Open your pussy portal to sunlight (A cleansing for your tastiest, most sacred
mystery)|No metaphors of flowers allowed

All living things need sunlight—no surprise there! And no surprise that the body
needs sunlight, even if that body has to be covered in a floppy hat and sunscreen,
but most people forget that their genitals need sunlight as well. Sit your ass on
the earth's throne. When I'm being really intentional, I like to get the earth's
permission, "may *I sit this assss on ya?*"Here I was in a public park, but a
beloved found some isolated space where I could air out, royally receive, and
charge up the light within! Mmm, beautiful beings of light, I draped my body in
such a way that if someone showed up unexpectedly, I could cover myself and
continue on with the moment. But here's the magic: As many times as I have
been nude in nature, I have never been "caught" once!! HA! Perhaps because I
commanded my safety and invisibility within my visibility! I commanded my

higher self–the love essence within me–to affirm my safety. And I removed my garments with such agency, freedom, and pleasure!! 'No fears allowed in this moment...'I told my whole self! Then I opened my legs, parted my lips (both sets), and just breathed, chile! Tip: You must open those inner lips too! Get a lil tan on your pussy and ride the energy of the wind. *Oh goodness it feels delicious to be entered in this way.* Gently bounce your ass and hips as you decree your grounding. Get 'high' off your own body's ecstasy. Slap your ass to shake the toxins out of your root.DEEPLY ride this sacred penetration for the wellness of your body, your life, your community, and the goodness of humanity!! You're going to get deliriously wet, just consider getting used to being wet daily, hourly in many cases. '*Let thou waters flow and blow into the earth.*'This moment is a holy scripture of unconditional love, connected to all there is, so take the whole moment inside without any inhibitions! Then after you settle down, observe your afterglow and share it with someone you adore! And that person will go into the world sharing bits of that transferred glow and on and on. We are all just that connected! Glory be to the Goddess who lives within us ALL!

CXCIII

Traveling around, moving about, and getting acclimated to a different way of living —new cities, new territories, new languages, new mountains, new islands, and new ways of doing similar things is a steady rebirthing process. It has been the purest form of non-attachment living (and loving), strengthening my capacity to be vulnerable, surrendering, light in mind but wild in body, sensitive, space-activating, intuitive, and aware. It's been a ringing freedom and quiet wisdom. I am reminded of the brilliancy of living inside an activated body temple and creating my life from that space of unlimited power without worry or concern. And that "I don't know" is truly an acceptable answer. Because I wake up ... and truly don't know but always trust that all is well. And surely it is.

Blooming Tip

An Activated Body is Generational Wealth

Living inside an activated body is generational wealth. Every ancestor lives in your blood and bones, therefore as you heal, you heal generations and generations to come. Any lover that enters your body immediately becomes financially, metaphysically, and physically wealthier. Their finances expand as they become brighter magnets to their goals, visions, dreams, and projects. Their skin clears up and body generally works better. Ask any one of my ex-lovers (past, present, and future), they may tell you if they were to be honest. *smiles*

Taking time to care for your body or activating your body is infinite wealth. The courage to live inside an activated body with activated lungs, appendages, breasts, ear lobes, mouth portals, and yoni portals is living prosperity. Courage because you evolve into your feminine wildness, dangerous to structure, normality, and conventional thinking, and being controlled in any way. You feed yourself daily pleasures because you know that pleasure fuels wealth. Nourishing your body with kind touch, words of affirmation, inviting (more) nature to come live inside you, taking time to prepare your meals and juices with intention and honor, being emotionally authentic and intelligent, attracting ways to move intense emotions out of the body, and reducing stressors are impetuses to infinite wealth, which includes but isn't limited to, generational wealth. Embodying love is the high art of infinite wealth. Doing what you love daily and finding ways to make a living off what you love are lifestyles of the infinite wealthy. If I decide to work outside of myself, I only work at places that I love. And my food/nutrient bill is $700/800 per month and my rent is $500 per month. I don't play those games; I know where my wealth lies.

CXCIV

When you discover your passions
you will have to make an effort to engage them daily.
These tuning forks to your life-force energy are your magic tools needed to truly bloom the Goddess archetype within you.

Holy Passions

Actualizing your passions is much larger than you,
because no one else has the cellular structure to do what you do in
the capacity that you do it.
Indeed it's the greatest contribution to eternal existence
to not give up on your visions and dreams.
Love needs that from you.
The people need that from you.
The rivers need that from you.
The animals need that from you.
Magic needs that from you.
The Infinite All and The Great Mystery need that from you.
The seeds, roots, water, and soil need that from you.
Because the harvest is within you.

Blooming Tip

The Goddess emerges in the silence
and blooms in The Great Mystery.
Just go forth Goddess.
Honor your alone time.
Observe the quiet.
Wear your black lace veil
and minister to the silence.
Be that beauty in the pitch black dark.
No need to explain yourself.

Ever.

Getting off social media, turning off the phone, not checking emails, turning off radio, sitting, coloring, painting toes, receiving a wheatgrass enema, making juices, wearing jewels, crowning the hair, laying up with a tree, listening, and doing nothing else. That's my feminine practice.

 What's your feminine practice? Because we are all practicing something.

CXCV

We don't need to wait for the experience of childbirth to participate in shifting mass consciousness expectations around birth. We have been programmed to think of the worst unimaginable pain when women give birth. What if it was all a belief set in motion by the past sex-negative, patriarchal paradigm? What if that *feeling* was put in place by a system that wished to diminish women's powers and desires to give birth naturally ... and pleasurably? What if the truth is that giving birth is and (has always inherently been) orgasmic beyond belief?

Orgasmic birthing

CXCVI

There is nothing more extraordinary than talking with someone who you have loved ... and made love to for years ... and still feeling intense passion over the human connection, the soul reconnection, the memory of sharing food and belly laughs, and that voice at 'hello.' My best lovers showed up in my 30s. While very few, all were just so exquisite, richly beautiful, worthy of celebration and praise. With this connection, how on earth does one ever "fall out of love?" Forever and forever I will always be there. Embodied, throned, pursed lip, perched, arched, and shaking in my spine over the memories. In love. Rising in love. Loving and being loved in a very special way. Cheers to the "exes," for they are never gone from any lover! One single thought WILL INDEED fire the synapses in the brain and CAN send pleasurable chemicals throughout the body, but only when thoughts of your ex *induce deep joy or can be transformed into joy and some brand of pleasure*. Reframing the story is a helpful tool to utilize here.

Consider embracing the exes, as you embrace new lovers—allow the oxytocin to flow through you and around you. And enjoy the resulting pleasure and added magnetism in your body.

I learned to adore my lovers' exes too. Mirrors in transition. Charred pieces of the other illuminated. ALL of us somehow intertwined into ONE: physically, mentally, emotionally, and (potentially) lovingly ... when we choose to do so.

ex-factor for life

CXCVII

Oftentimes
when I am cleaning floors,
yes,
cleaning ... floors...,
I am doing so
with full joy
and sensual delight.
Grateful to be in
a healthy red clay body
with knees that bend
without fail
and
a spine that curls
when commanded.
Nude or
barely covered.
Juicy and ignited.
Cleaning
floors with my bare brown hands
and freshly-washed white towels.
No mop, please.
Only Thelonious Monk
blasting from speakers
and homemade
lemon soap heightening
my senses.
I am mopping
floors with my bare hands.
Receiving information.
Interpreting corners.
Feeling my way into orgasm.
Creating my own pleasures!
Imprinting the past.
Remembering and reconstructing...
Needlessly to say I *love* clean floors!

Cleaning floors/The pleasure principle

CXCVIII

Just because you are sitting with sexual energy in your body temple, even if you are connected to a person in that moment, doesn't mean that the energy has to be organized and directed into a sexual experience. Sexual energy is the most potent energy on the planet—it creates life and BRINGS life to everything. You can allow that energy to run wild, shake open your chakra fruits (healing your organs), and spill just a little bit of juice everywhere. That's your power and gift to yourself and the world. Consider the desire to cultivate your sexual energy inside and outside the context of another person. Because it's more than just sex; it's life force. It means that your body is alive and activated and healthy and free.

~Cultivate your sexual energy~

CXCIX

Gold particles, wild passionate sweetness, magic, honey, movement, balance, multidimensional, healthy aura, trance, chakras bursting, transformation, abundance, healing, synchronicity, nature, water, at least 7 OR MORE senses engaged to produce all sorts of minerals, vitamins, and pleasurable chemicals in the body temple: Consider what happens to the planet if ALL lovemaking carried elements of Oshun or any other Goddess of Love to it.

 Goddess of love-making

cc

Masturbation
is one way to procure sacred information
from the higher self.

When masturbating, wear
your cowry shells. Crown your head or hair.
frankincense. myrrh. flower petals. ankle bells.
painted toes. yoni egg. fabric
spray your thighs. with rose water and ylang ylang.
drown the sheets in your aromatherapeutic waters.

Listen. Receive. Let it go.

Cum loudly; The information is encoded in the orgasm.

 **Master bait**

CCI

Can you guess what's going on here? I'm actually clearing my throat chakra, beautifying my skin, and becoming younger with every lick and suck. Licking in conjunction with sucking produces enzymes in the mouth and throat, enzymes that help the body to breakdown and digest nutrients. One of keys to healthy skin and wonderfully healthy pussy lies in the body's ability to digest necessary nutrients. Some women take vitamins (yay for food-based vitamins!) but are unable to receive any nutrients from their supplements or even the healthy foods and juices they intake because their bodies do not have the proper enzymes and probiotics to break down whatever's being consumed. Plus there is the added value of ingesting nutrients of the cucumber after it's been licked and sucked. You see how all this is connected?

Cucumber Medicine

CCII

Mum taught me to put frozen cucumbers on any skin blemishes and flare ups...

so here I am 20 years later.

Steps: Squeeze the cucumber juice into the skin. Then sing to the body temple. Simple, eh?!

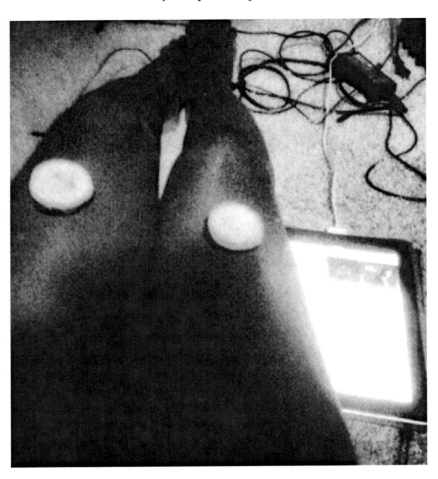

CCIII

SET ASIDE ONE DAY A WEEK FOR BEAUTY RITUALS. WEAR A HOMEMADE CROWN. SOAK YOUR FEET. EXFOLIATE YOUR KNEES AND ELBOWS. SCRUB THE BACK OF YOUR NECK. TEND TO YOUR GUM TISSUES. STEAM YOUR PUSSY. TOUCH THOSE PARTS NEEDING THE MOST ATTENTION AND PRAISE. YOU IN ALL YOUR UNSHAKEABLE DIVINITY AND WILD CHARM ARE SO WORTHY OF THE DEVOTION AND EXALTATION.

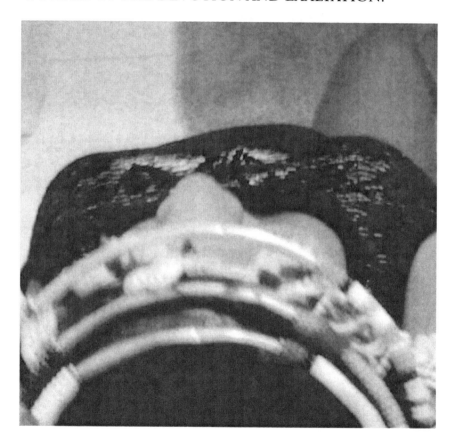

CCIV

My all-time favorite beauty ritual: dry skin brushing

There are a myriad of benefits to dry skin brushing! The part that I'm most attracted to is that it reduces the appearance of cellulite or eliminates it altogether. There is ABSOLUTELY nothing "wrong" with cellulite—lovely lady tiger stripes are beautiful! But there are some women who are interested in softening or removing their cellulite. For those women, read on!

I have been consistently skin-brushing since 2004, at least 5 times a week, so needlessly to say, skin-brushing is indeed a ritual for me.

What is dry skin-brushing you ask!?!

It's using a natural brush (a dry natural brush) to GENTLY brush your skin into the softest, clearest surrender.

264

Steps to 3-5 minutes of dry-brushing
(Brush at least once a day before shower/bath)

1. Purchase a natural brush from any natural foods store or online natural retailer. Do your research!

1. Set personal intentions. Command your brush to meet your needs and desires for your body temple.

2. Start at your feet and brush in circular motions up towards your heart. As you pass each major chakra point (flowers), visualize the colors associated with each chakra and command each flower petals to open and clear. You may even turn red or look a little ashy. That's perfect!

When dry-brushing your ass, bend over and get in there really good. Make sensual moves. Harness a connection with your brush. Trust your brush to be of service to you.

Remember you are not just dry-brushing your skin, you are activating your whole being. Brush like it. Let the brushing make you smile, moan, giggle ... essentially feel the brush.

Lets brush up on our wombs!

Our wombs are the stargate in which life or dreams or projects are born. A creative vortex of spirituality, wisdom, and sensuality. Among many things, the womb is the epicenter of her inner security, a sacred space that can be leaned upon at any time and return to for endless replenishment and support. It is the foundation that provides abundant nurturing for a woman's heart to open. A home base of perpetual, timeless, spaceless, ancient wisdom and embodiments of royal deliciousness. One of the best things you could do for your transformation is to tap into your mystery. Get to know your dark magic. Your sacred gateway of love, offering your lover a place to return to for rest and nourishment. A transformer and transmuter of all energy out of alignment with love. You, Darlin', have that capacity within you. Vast. Infinite. Eternal. Immortal. A quiet, cauldron of Source energy. Roll out the red carpet. And twirl!

CCV

Abundance lies

in our capacity to cultivate

love and adoration for our body temples, realizing

that the magic and healing we seek

*can only truly **live within***

and radiate outwards.

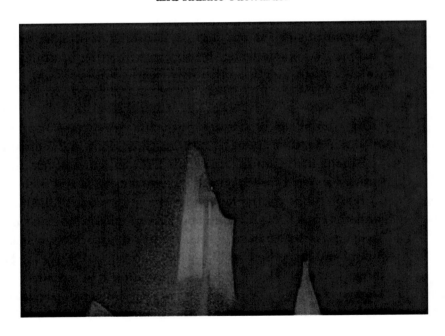

FEMININE FOODS

Papaya

Cucumber

Free-range eggs

Watermelon (Juiced only)

Mango

Oranges

Cantaloupe

Honeydew Melon

Avocado

Kiwi

Squash

Kumquat

Prunes

Raw milk

Apple

Blueberries, raspberries, strawberries

Carrot

Lettuce

Cabbage

Radish

Turnip

Spinach

Celery

Broccoli

Sweet Potato

Lentils

Tomato

Garlic

Pomegranate

Peaches

Wild Salmon

Warm water

Cultured yogurt

Cinnamon

Honey

(all organically and locally grown as much as possible)

Feminine foods usher the body into calmness, suppleness, and ease.

The Harvest

In China, female ejaculation is called "moon flower medicine." Get that download into your body temple! Mmm. Lets sip one for preventative care! Just remember when you bloom, you will bloom in every area of your life. I cultivated my moon flower medicine in late 2013. Frankly I just LOVE witnessing the abundance of water releasing from my body temple, further confirmation that my self-work is healing my body, healing the bodies of those I encounter, and transforming lives. As a result of reframing my stories and evolving beyond my learnings, perceived limitations, and continuing to challenge my fears, I have bloomed in a myriad of ways....and YOU CAN TOO. Go on, Goddess. Let your waters flow. The world needs your brand of healing. ♥

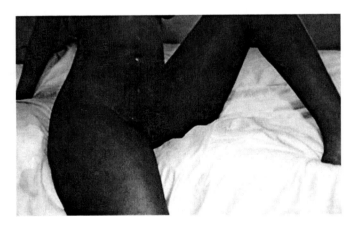

One heart,
India Ame'ye

You Look Like Something Blooming: <u>Your healing is the collective's healing</u>

Life is sweetly simplistic: We are all simply turning into the energies we are tuning into.

Don't ever apologize for your creative space or silence. Sometimes I think the only people who understand writers are ... other creatives, particularly other creatives who are serious about publishing their work. You never really have to explain anything to these folks. You need time to yourself and sitting down at the base of a tree, doing nothing, is sometimes a part of the creative process.

<u>Please support your independent artists, if not me, then someone else for sure!</u>

Hi Luscious Reader, THANK YOU FOR YOUR PURCHASE!

Thank you for your patience! Thank you for being love's reflection. And thank you for believing in this sacred work.

Thank you!!!!

Nature's magic, Fertility, The Moon and moonblood, Oshun, Oya-Olowo, Deer, Aja, Ogun, Lakshmi, Artemis, Frida K., Miriam Mum, Mom Mary, Aunt Gem, Sherry, Mary Magdalene, Josephine B., Kali, The sacred feminine and masculine wholeness, Ms. Lavern, Uzomaka, D., Kenya K Stevens, Denise, Tasha W., Saudade, Kerline, Billie; Netherina and Francine, Monica B., Janice Phillips, Arielle, Adinah M., Seraphina, Hadiiya B., Valencia W., Christina H., Soraya, Rev Goddess Charmaine, Shawn D., Tajh A., Nut Butterfly, Nina L., Saudade, Fiona Z., Patsy Peajae, Deborah H., Ebele A., Tonya K., Makeda S., Soy F., Maisha A., Keenyah Elle; Makeda Smith; Nayyirah W., Mwau'L Womb, Dommy Mars, Ayo Fuega, Honeybush A., Lesley L., Deborah B., De'Arcy B., Alex S., Tiffany B., DaniElle, Tiara K., Valerie C., Sunshine C., LaShanna B., DaniElle, Lesley Love, Adriana, Bridget C., Shine B., Aaron-Sade, LadyShepsa J., Jetia D., Ama., Asha D., Clinton L., Tasha S., Raquel H., YokoOno W., Korby, Princess C., Pamela O., Namaste, Shira, Aheri, Graceful Empowerment, Nev N., Chelsie B., Surya D., Tiffany OrganicBlood, S. Badiyah, Julie M., Helese, Gebrina, Billie J., Angel A., Tajh A., Dommy M., Gebrina, Iyalosa O., Surya, Kissiah, Christa, Brianna M., Phaedra C., Deborah B., L'erin, LaTasha G., Tonya W., Devi W., Audrey H., Gail H., Hasina, Makeda V., Maryoi, Ifini, and the lovers and partners (past, present, and future) in my life. Any person whose name is not listed but contributed monetarily or in spirit, ***please forgive my oversight. I love you all! Thank you deeply, etherically, and eternally.***

OPEN AIR

In what ways are you blooming in your life (garden) and body (temple)? Write your notes here. Jot down anything that came up from you?

_____

_____

_____

_____

_____

_____

_____

_____

_____

_____

_____

_____

_____

Once you "know," you have the responsibility of sharing with someone else. Share what you learned with a friend.

"Every time a woman has an orgasm, the patriarchy cracks." -Lisa C.

Dedicated to *All* Women

You can do it

YOU ARE THE HARVEST.

MADE OF STARS AND THE EARTH'S DELIGHT.

THE FULL BLOOM

CARRYING THE FULL MOON.

HEALING YOUR ORGANS THROUGH THE NEW MOON

AND TRANSFORMING YOUR LIFE IN THE FULL MOON.

THANK YOU FOR YOUR SERVICES.

Thank you Darlin' for reading and observing my sacred work over the years. I hold divine expectation that my book of charms will be a nourishing resource to help unearth potent divine feminine wholeness and integrative cellular transformation within us all. The ponds, lakes, rivers, and oceanic bodies of water surely need it. Every single human body needs it. The collective body deeply needs it. In Yeye's Name!!

CPSIA information can be obtained at www.ICGtesting.com
Printed in the USA
LVOW06s2159050815

449049LV00012B/237/P